COURTNEY CRUMRIN IN THE TWILIGHT KINGDOM™

for Julie and for Corinne

Courtney Crumrin in the Twilight Kingdom™

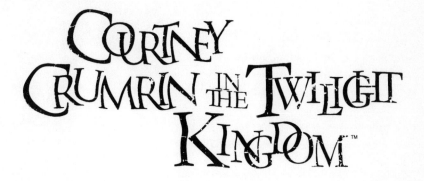

By Ted Naifeh

Design by
Ted Naifeh
with assistance from Steven Birch @ Servo

Edited by
Joe Nozemack & James Lucas Jones

Published by Oni Press, Inc.
Joe Nozemack, publisher
James Lucas Jones, senior editor
Randal C. Jarrell, managing editor
Ian Shaughnessy, editorial assistant

This collects issues 1-4 of the Oni Press comics series *Courtney Crumrin in the Twilight Kingdom*.

ONI PRESS, INC.
6336 SE Milwaukie Avenue, PMB 30
Portland, OR 97202
USA

www.onipress.com
www.tednaifeh.com

First edition: September 2004
ISBN 1-932664-01-7

3 5 7 9 10 8 6 4
PRINTED IN CANADA.

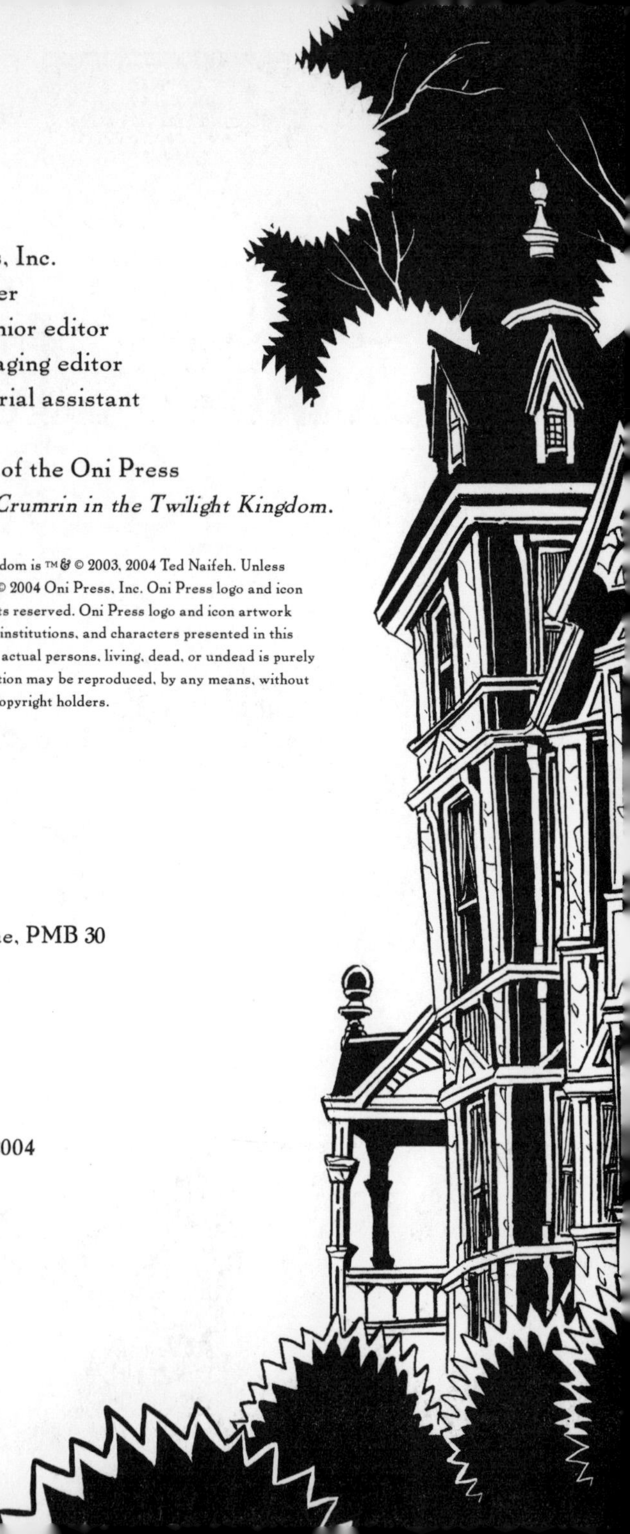

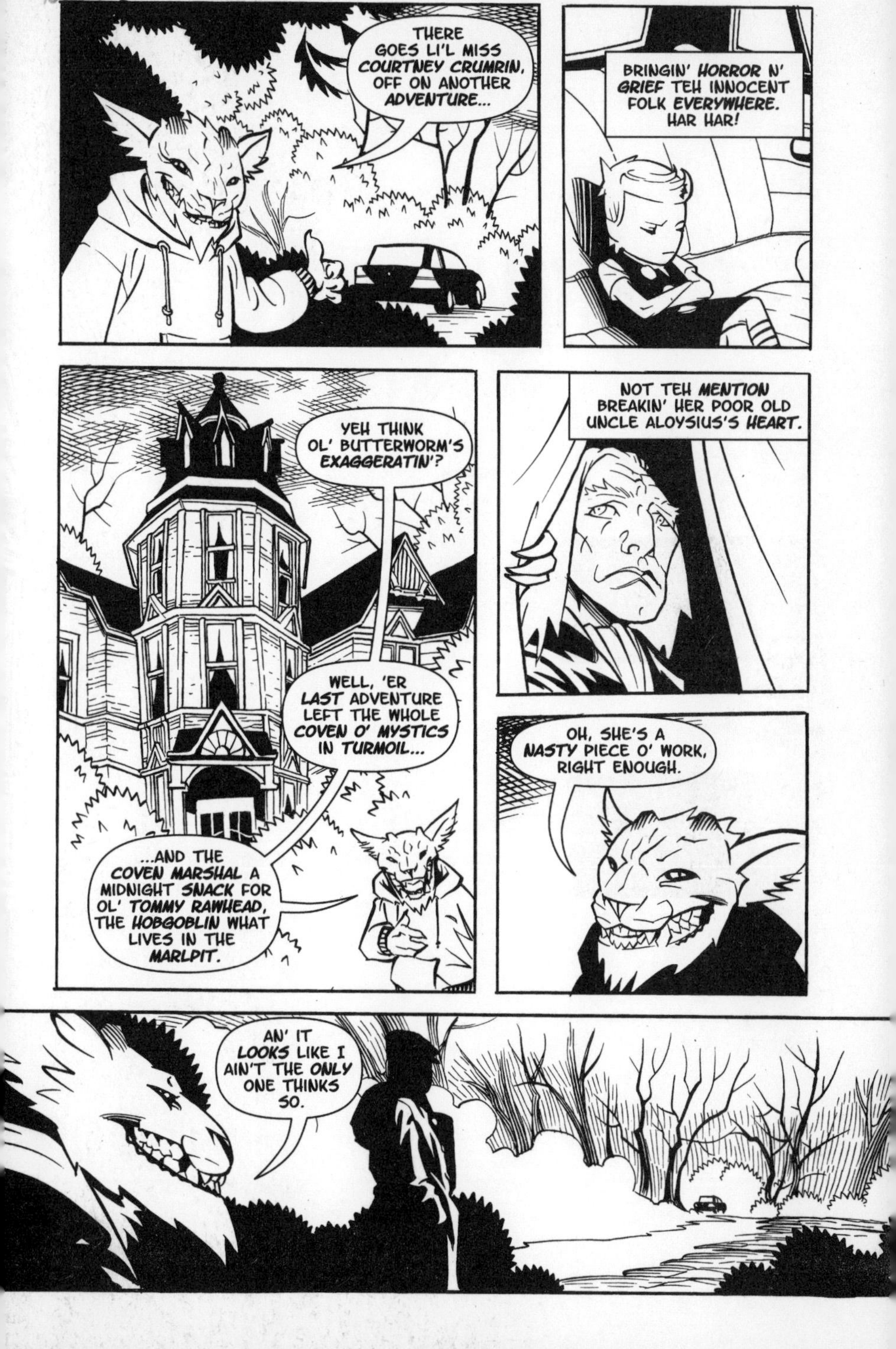

THERE GOES LI'L MISS COURTNEY CRUMRIN, OFF ON ANOTHER ADVENTURE...
BRINGIN' HORROR N' GRIEF TEH INNOCENT FOLK EVERYWHERE. HAR HAR!
YEH THINK OL' BUTTERWORM'S EXAGGERATIN'?
WELL, 'ER LAST ADVENTURE LEFT THE WHOLE COVEN O' MYSTICS IN TURMOIL...
...AND THE COVEN MARSHAL A MIDNIGHT SNACK FOR OL' TOMMY RAWHEAD, THE HOBGOBLIN WHAT LIVES IN THE MARLPIT.
NOT TEH MENTION BREAKIN' HER POOR OLD UNCLE ALOYSIUS'S HEART.
OH, SHE'S A NASTY PIECE O' WORK, RIGHT ENOUGH.
AN' IT LOOKS LIKE I AIN'T THE ONLY ONE THINKS SO.

CHAPTER ONE

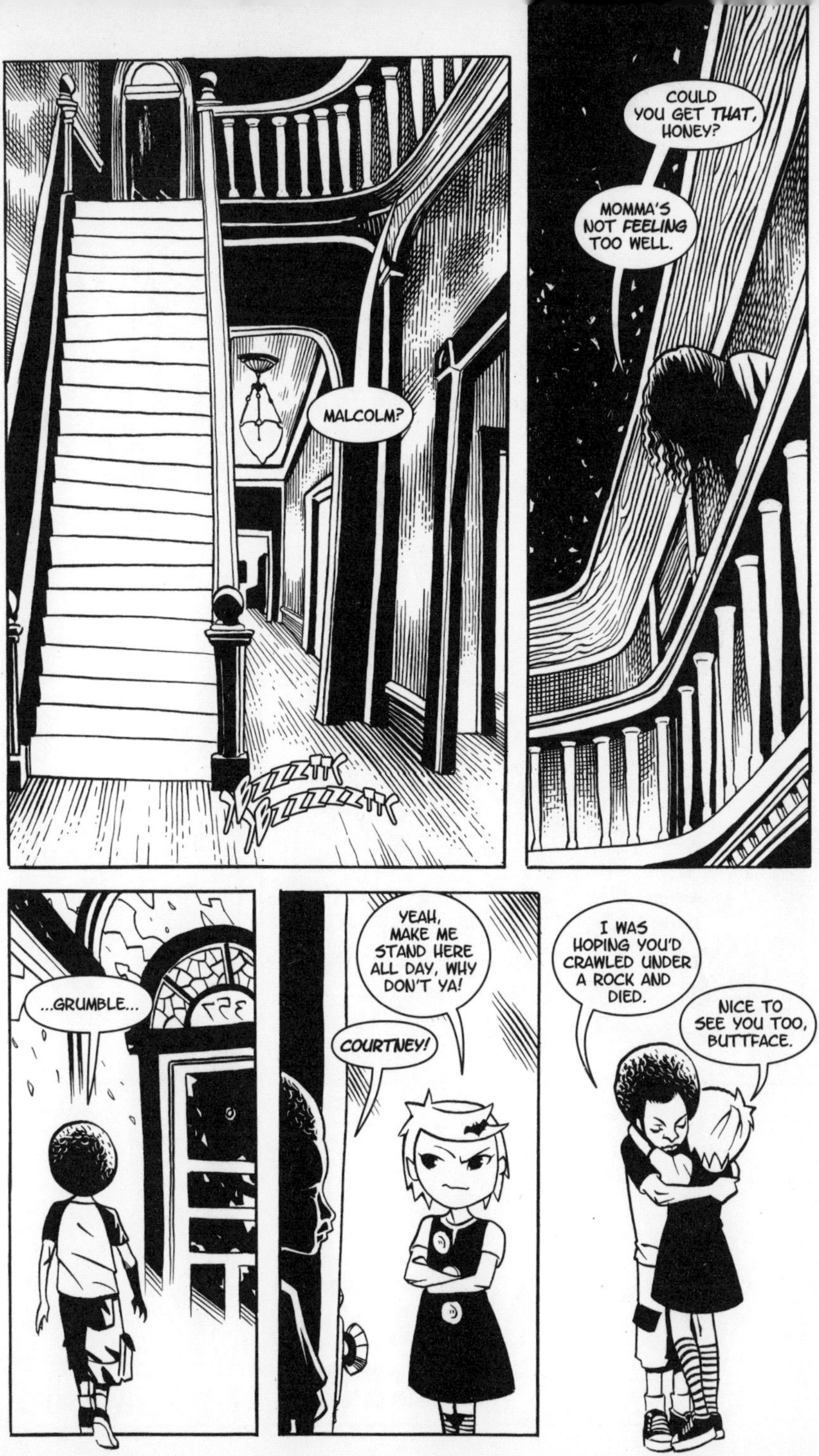
MALCOLM?
BZZZZZTTT
BZZZZZTTT
COULD YOU GET THAT, HONEY?
MOMMA'S NOT FEELING TOO WELL.
...GRUMBLE...
357
YEAH, MAKE ME STAND HERE ALL DAY, WHY DON'T YA!
COURTNEY!
I WAS HOPING YOU'D CRAWLED UNDER A ROCK AND DIED.
NICE TO SEE YOU TOO, BUTTFACE.

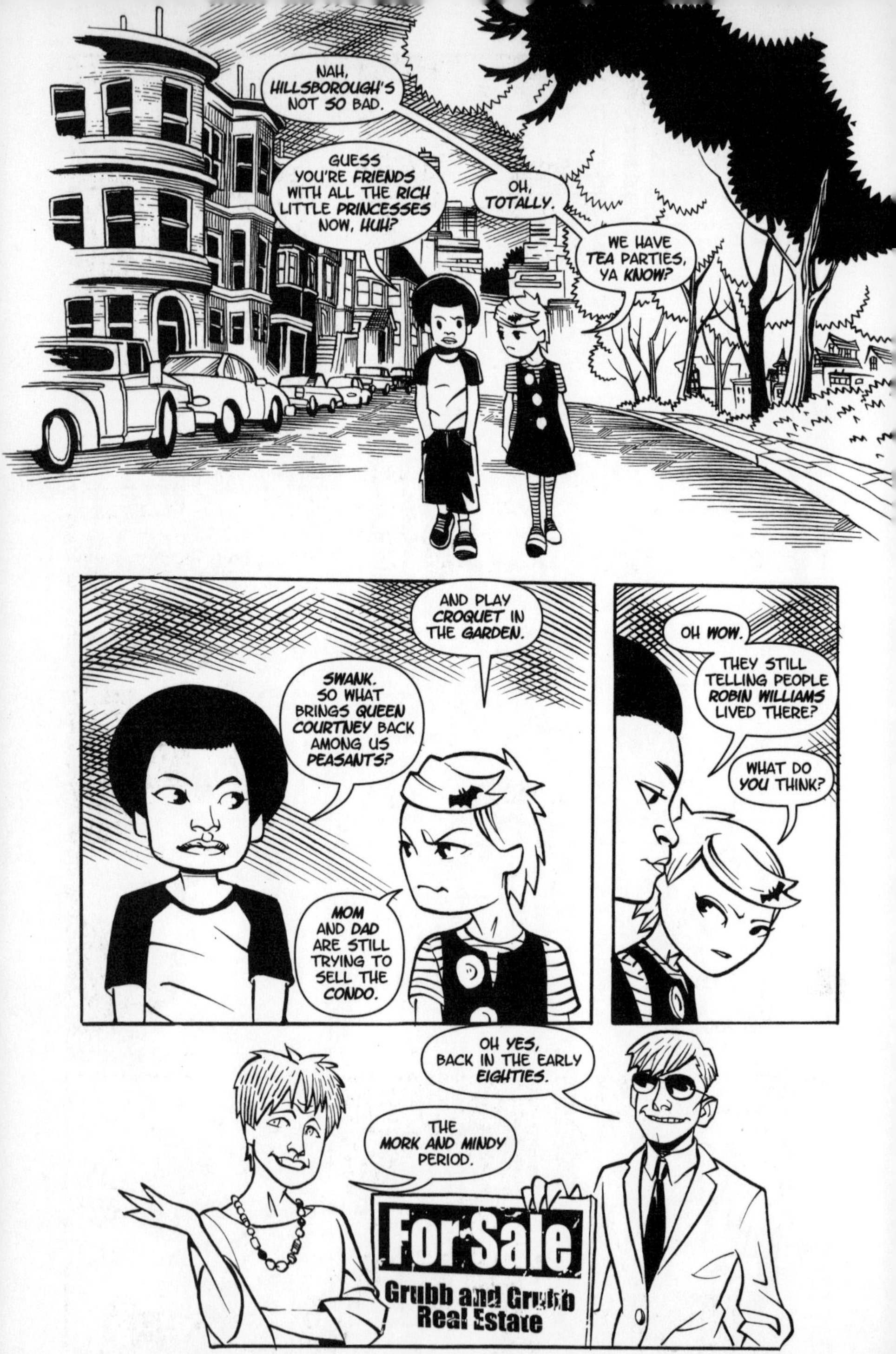
NAH, HILLSBOROUGH'S NOT SO BAD.
GUESS YOU'RE FRIENDS WITH ALL THE RICH LITTLE PRINCESSES NOW, HUH?
OH, TOTALLY.
WE HAVE TEA PARTIES, YA KNOW?
AND PLAY CROQUET IN THE GARDEN.
SWANK. SO WHAT BRINGS QUEEN COURTNEY BACK AMONG US PEASANTS?
MOM AND DAD ARE STILL TRYING TO SELL THE CONDO.
OH WOW.
THEY STILL TELLING PEOPLE ROBIN WILLIAMS LIVED THERE?
WHAT DO YOU THINK?
OH YES, BACK IN THE EARLY EIGHTIES.
THE MORK AND MINDY PERIOD.
For Sale
Grubb and Grubb
Real Estate

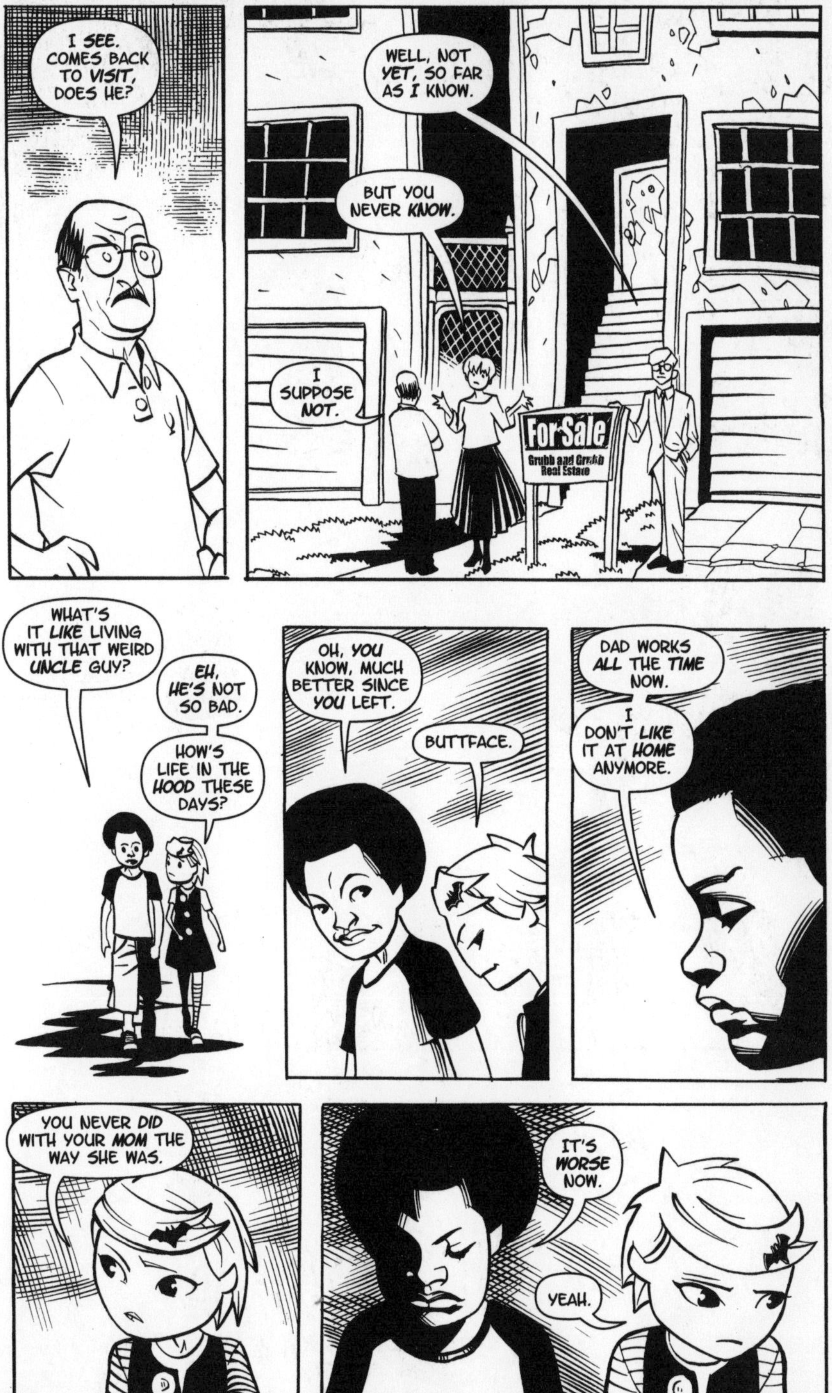
I SEE. COMES BACK TO VISIT, DOES HE?
WELL, NOT YET, SO FAR AS I KNOW.
BUT YOU NEVER KNOW.
I SUPPOSE NOT.
For Sale
Grubb and Grubb Real Estate
WHAT'S IT LIKE LIVING WITH THAT WEIRD UNCLE GUY?
EH, HE'S NOT SO BAD.
HOW'S LIFE IN THE HOOD THESE DAYS?
OH, YOU KNOW, MUCH BETTER SINCE YOU LEFT.
BUTTFACE.
DAD WORKS ALL THE TIME NOW.
I DON'T LIKE IT AT HOME ANYMORE.
YOU NEVER DID WITH YOUR MOM THE WAY SHE WAS.
IT'S WORSE NOW.
YEAH.

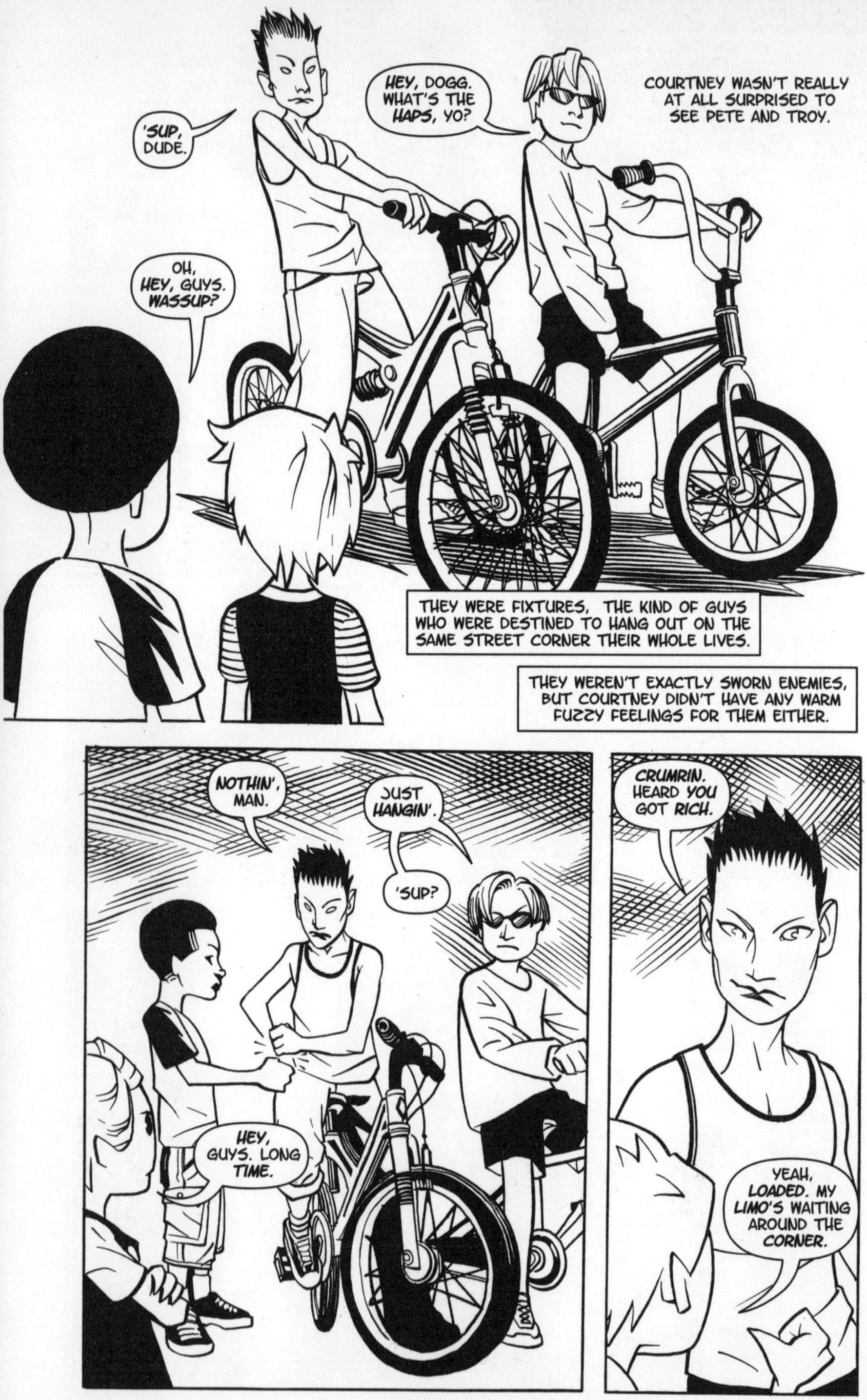

COURTNEY WASN'T REALLY AT ALL SURPRISED TO SEE PETE AND TROY.
HEY, DOGG. WHAT'S THE HAPS, YO?
'SUP, DUDE.
OH, HEY, GUYS. WASSUP?
THEY WERE FIXTURES, THE KIND OF GUYS WHO WERE DESTINED TO HANG OUT ON THE SAME STREET CORNER THEIR WHOLE LIVES.
THEY WEREN'T EXACTLY SWORN ENEMIES, BUT COURTNEY DIDN'T HAVE ANY WARM FUZZY FEELINGS FOR THEM EITHER.
NOTHIN', MAN.
JUST HANGIN'.
'SUP?
HEY, GUYS. LONG TIME.
CRUMRIN. HEARD YOU GOT RICH.
YEAH, LOADED. MY LIMO'S WAITING AROUND THE CORNER.

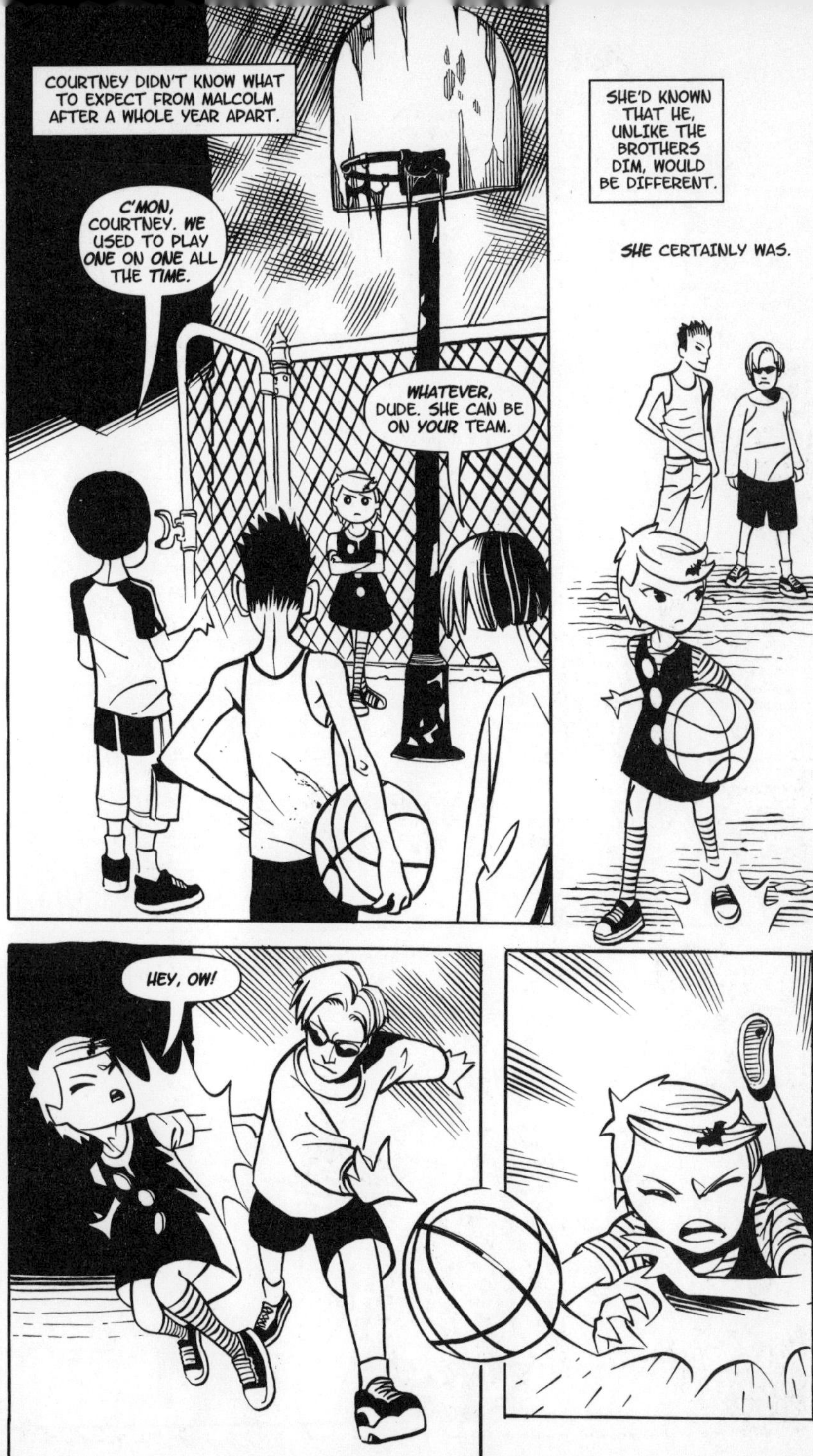
COURTNEY DIDN'T KNOW WHAT TO EXPECT FROM MALCOLM AFTER A WHOLE YEAR APART.
C'MON, COURTNEY. WE USED TO PLAY ONE ON ONE ALL THE TIME.
WHATEVER, DUDE. SHE CAN BE ON YOUR TEAM.
SHE'D KNOWN THAT HE, UNLIKE THE BROTHERS DIM, WOULD BE DIFFERENT.
SHE CERTAINLY WAS.
HEY, OW!

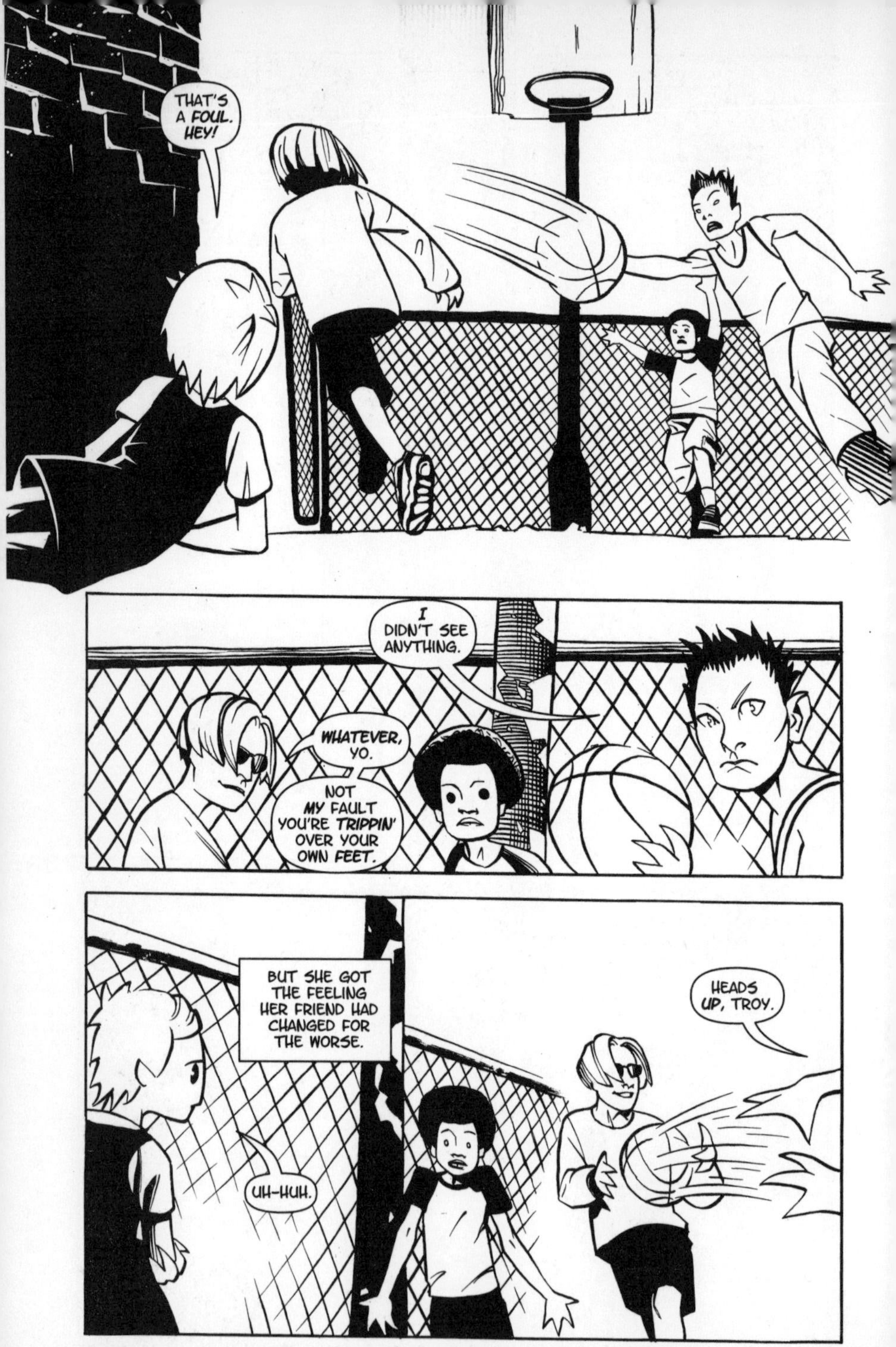
THAT'S A FOUL. HEY!
I DIDN'T SEE ANYTHING.
WHATEVER, YO.
NOT MY FAULT YOU'RE TRIPPIN' OVER YOUR OWN FEET.
BUT SHE GOT THE FEELING HER FRIEND HAD CHANGED FOR THE WORSE.
HEADS UP, TROY.
UH-HUH.

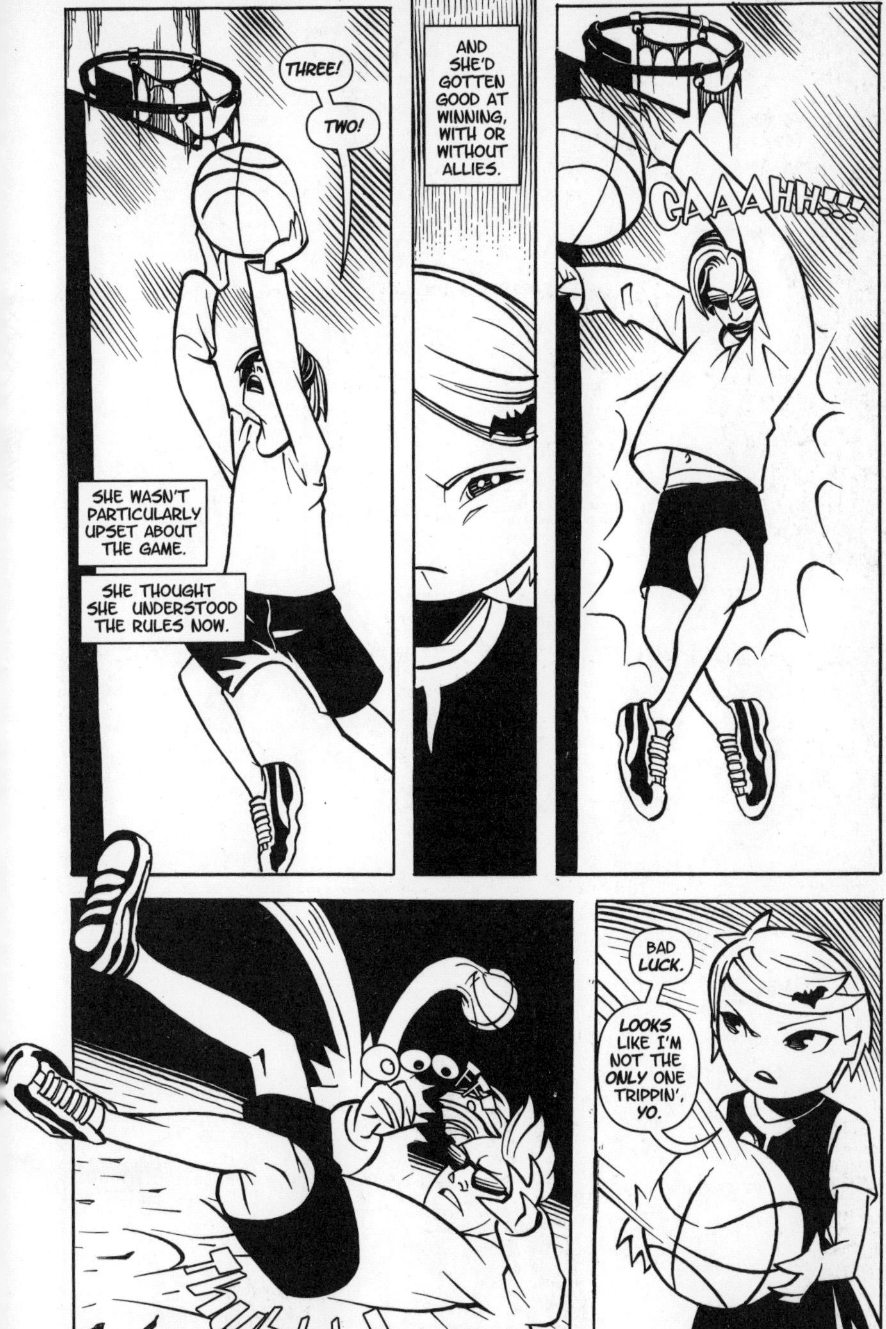
THREE!
TWO!
SHE WASN'T PARTICULARLY UPSET ABOUT THE GAME.
SHE THOUGHT SHE UNDERSTOOD THE RULES NOW.
AND SHE'D GOTTEN GOOD AT WINNING, WITH OR WITHOUT ALLIES.
GAAAHH!!!
THUBBB!
BAD LUCK.
LOOKS LIKE I'M NOT THE ONLY ONE TRIPPIN', YO.

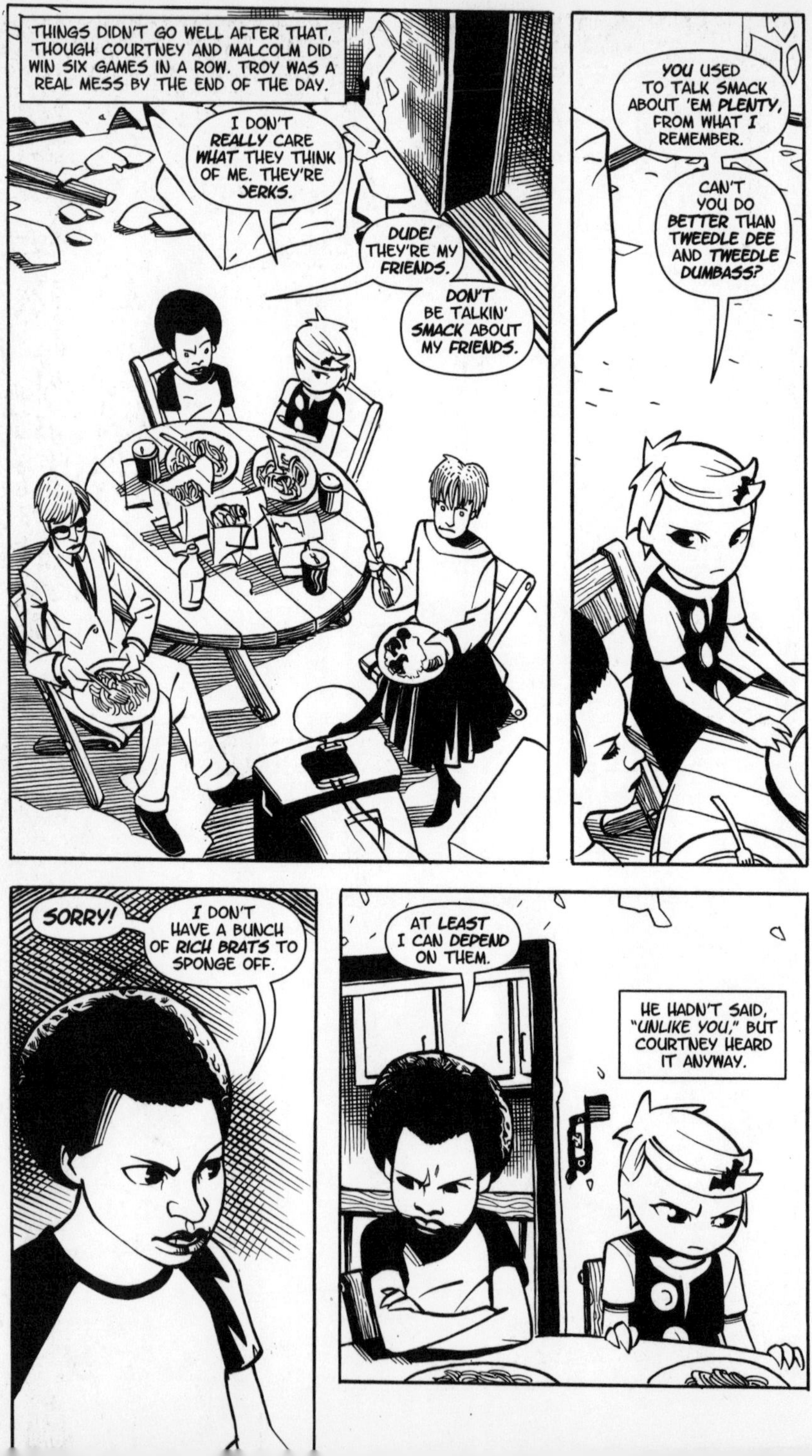
THINGS DIDN'T GO WELL AFTER THAT, THOUGH COURTNEY AND MALCOLM DID WIN SIX GAMES IN A ROW. TROY WAS A REAL MESS BY THE END OF THE DAY.
I DON'T REALLY CARE WHAT THEY THINK OF ME. THEY'RE JERKS.
DUDE! THEY'RE MY FRIENDS.
DON'T BE TALKIN' SMACK ABOUT MY FRIENDS.
YOU USED TO TALK SMACK ABOUT 'EM PLENTY, FROM WHAT I REMEMBER.
CAN'T YOU DO BETTER THAN TWEEDLE DEE AND TWEEDLE DUMBASS?
SORRY!
I DON'T HAVE A BUNCH OF RICH BRATS TO SPONGE OFF.
AT LEAST I CAN DEPEND ON THEM.
HE HADN'T SAID, "UNLIKE YOU," BUT COURTNEY HEARD IT ANYWAY.

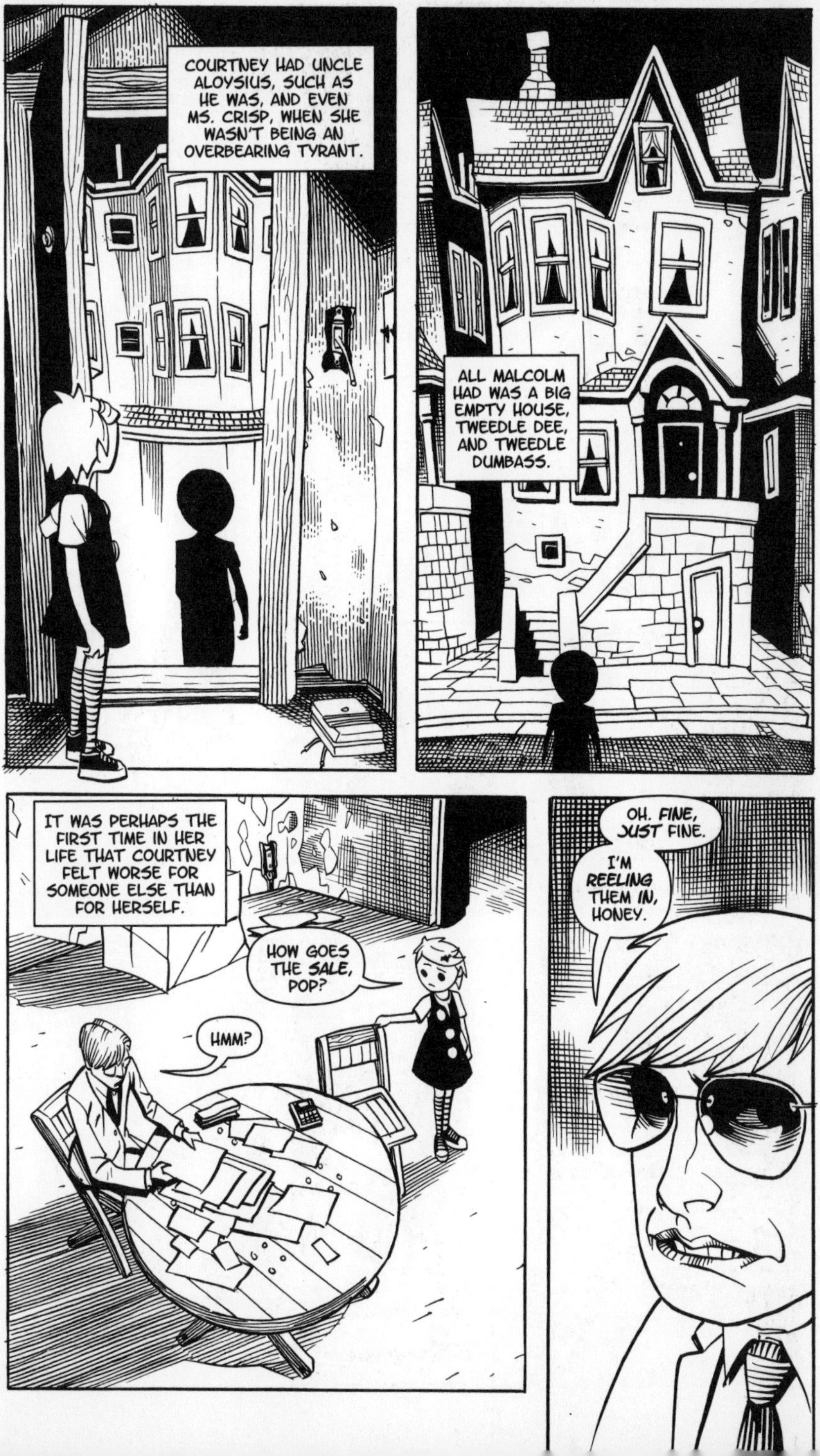
COURTNEY HAD UNCLE ALOYSIUS, SUCH AS HE WAS, AND EVEN MS. CRISP, WHEN SHE WASN'T BEING AN OVERBEARING TYRANT.
ALL MALCOLM HAD WAS A BIG EMPTY HOUSE, TWEEDLE DEE, AND TWEEDLE DUMBASS.
IT WAS PERHAPS THE FIRST TIME IN HER LIFE THAT COURTNEY FELT WORSE FOR SOMEONE ELSE THAN FOR HERSELF.
HOW GOES THE SALE, POP?
HMM?
OH. FINE, JUST FINE.
I'M REELING THEM IN, HONEY.

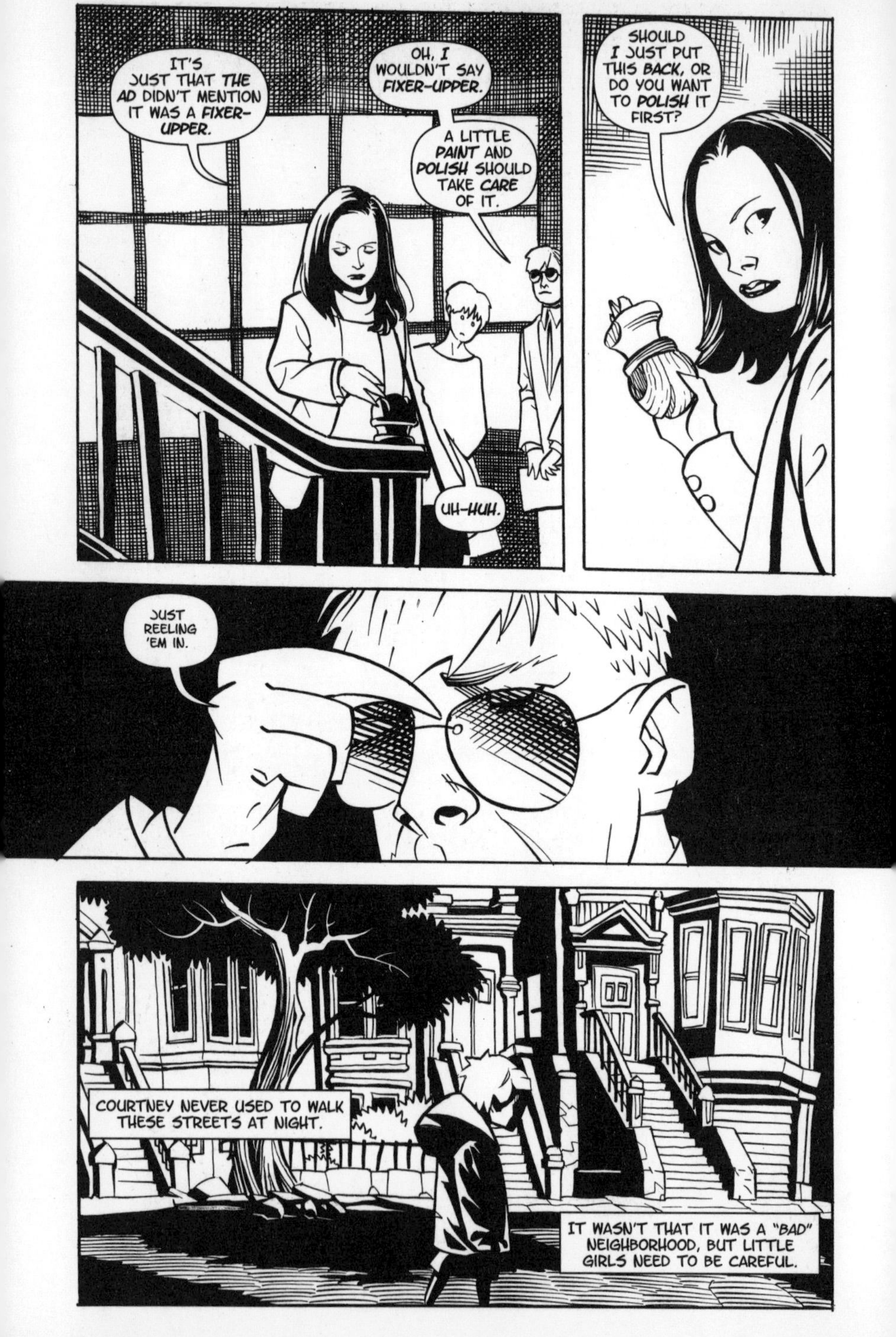
IT'S JUST THAT THE AD DIDN'T MENTION IT WAS A FIXER-UPPER.
OH, I WOULDN'T SAY FIXER-UPPER.
A LITTLE PAINT AND POLISH SHOULD TAKE CARE OF IT.
UH-HUH.
SHOULD I JUST PUT THIS BACK, OR DO YOU WANT TO POLISH IT FIRST?
JUST REELING 'EM IN.
COURTNEY NEVER USED TO WALK THESE STREETS AT NIGHT.
IT WASN'T THAT IT WAS A "BAD" NEIGHBORHOOD, BUT LITTLE GIRLS NEED TO BE CAREFUL.

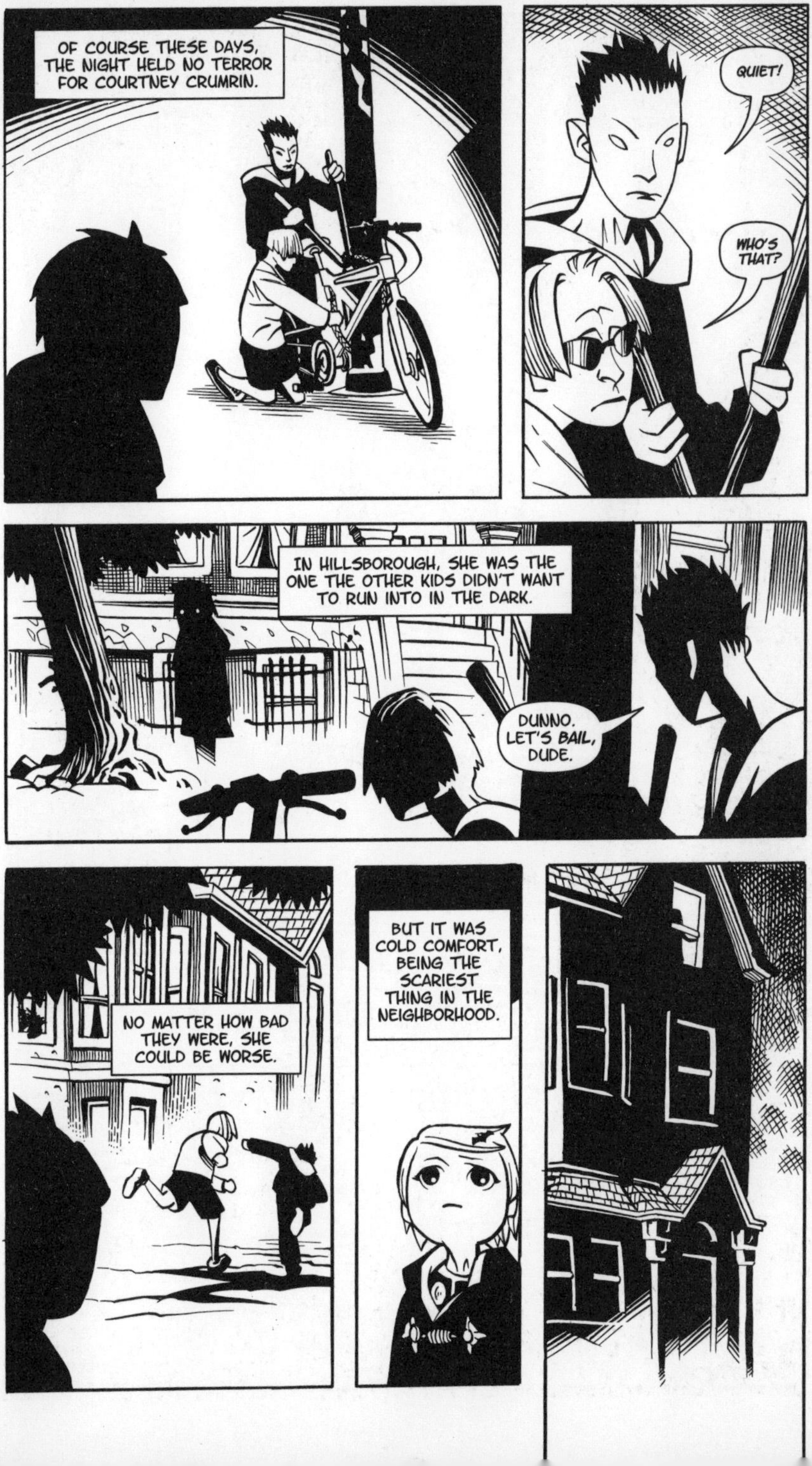
OF COURSE THESE DAYS, THE NIGHT HELD NO TERROR FOR COURTNEY CRUMRIN.
QUIET!
WHO'S THAT?
IN HILLSBOROUGH, SHE WAS THE ONE THE OTHER KIDS DIDN'T WANT TO RUN INTO IN THE DARK.
DUNNO. LET'S BAIL, DUDE.
NO MATTER HOW BAD THEY WERE, SHE COULD BE WORSE.
BUT IT WAS COLD COMFORT, BEING THE SCARIEST THING IN THE NEIGHBORHOOD.

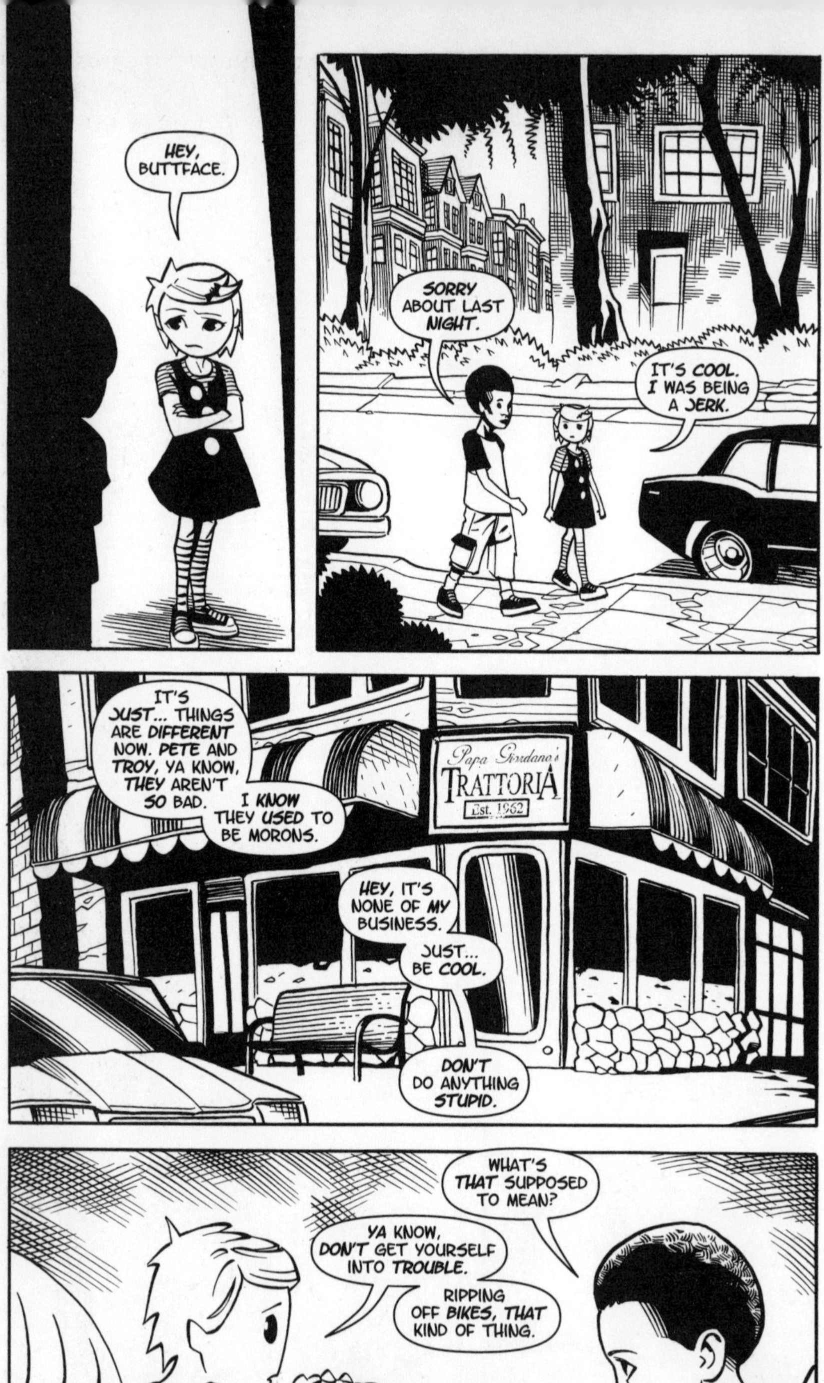
HEY, BUTTFACE.
SORRY ABOUT LAST NIGHT.
IT'S COOL. I WAS BEING A JERK.
IT'S JUST... THINGS ARE DIFFERENT NOW. PETE AND TROY, YA KNOW, THEY AREN'T SO BAD.
I KNOW THEY USED TO BE MORONS.
Papa Giordano's
TRATTORIA
Est. 1962
HEY, IT'S NONE OF MY BUSINESS.
JUST... BE COOL.
DON'T DO ANYTHING STUPID.
WHAT'S THAT SUPPOSED TO MEAN?
YA KNOW, DON'T GET YOURSELF INTO TROUBLE.
RIPPING OFF BIKES, THAT KIND OF THING.

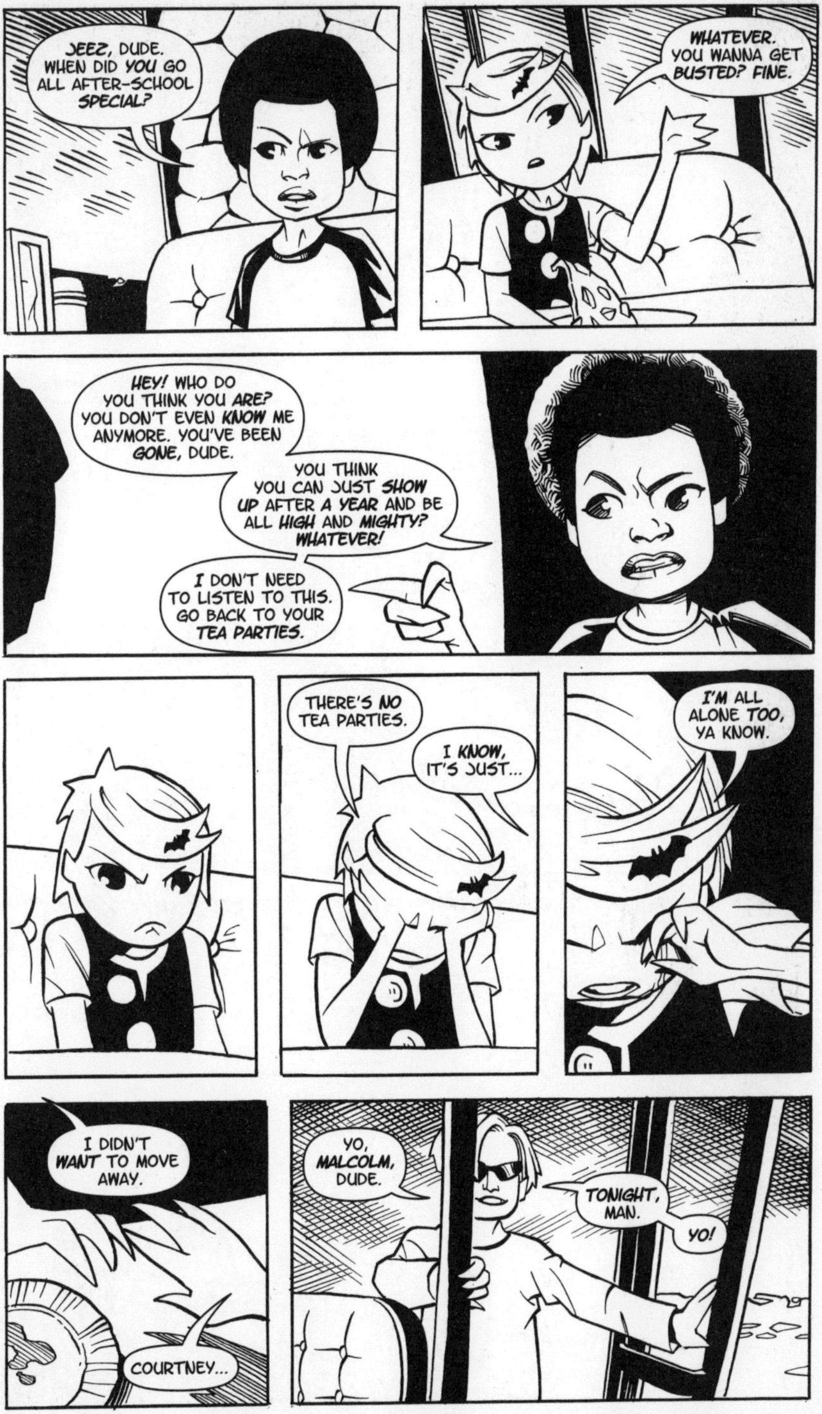
JEEZ, DUDE. WHEN DID YOU GO ALL AFTER-SCHOOL SPECIAL?
WHATEVER. YOU WANNA GET BUSTED? FINE.
HEY! WHO DO YOU THINK YOU ARE? YOU DON'T EVEN KNOW ME ANYMORE. YOU'VE BEEN GONE, DUDE.
YOU THINK YOU CAN JUST SHOW UP AFTER A YEAR AND BE ALL HIGH AND MIGHTY? WHATEVER!
I DON'T NEED TO LISTEN TO THIS. GO BACK TO YOUR TEA PARTIES.
THERE'S NO TEA PARTIES.
I KNOW, IT'S JUST...
I'M ALL ALONE TOO, YA KNOW.
I DIDN'T WANT TO MOVE AWAY.
COURTNEY...
YO, MALCOLM, DUDE.
TONIGHT, MAN.
YO!

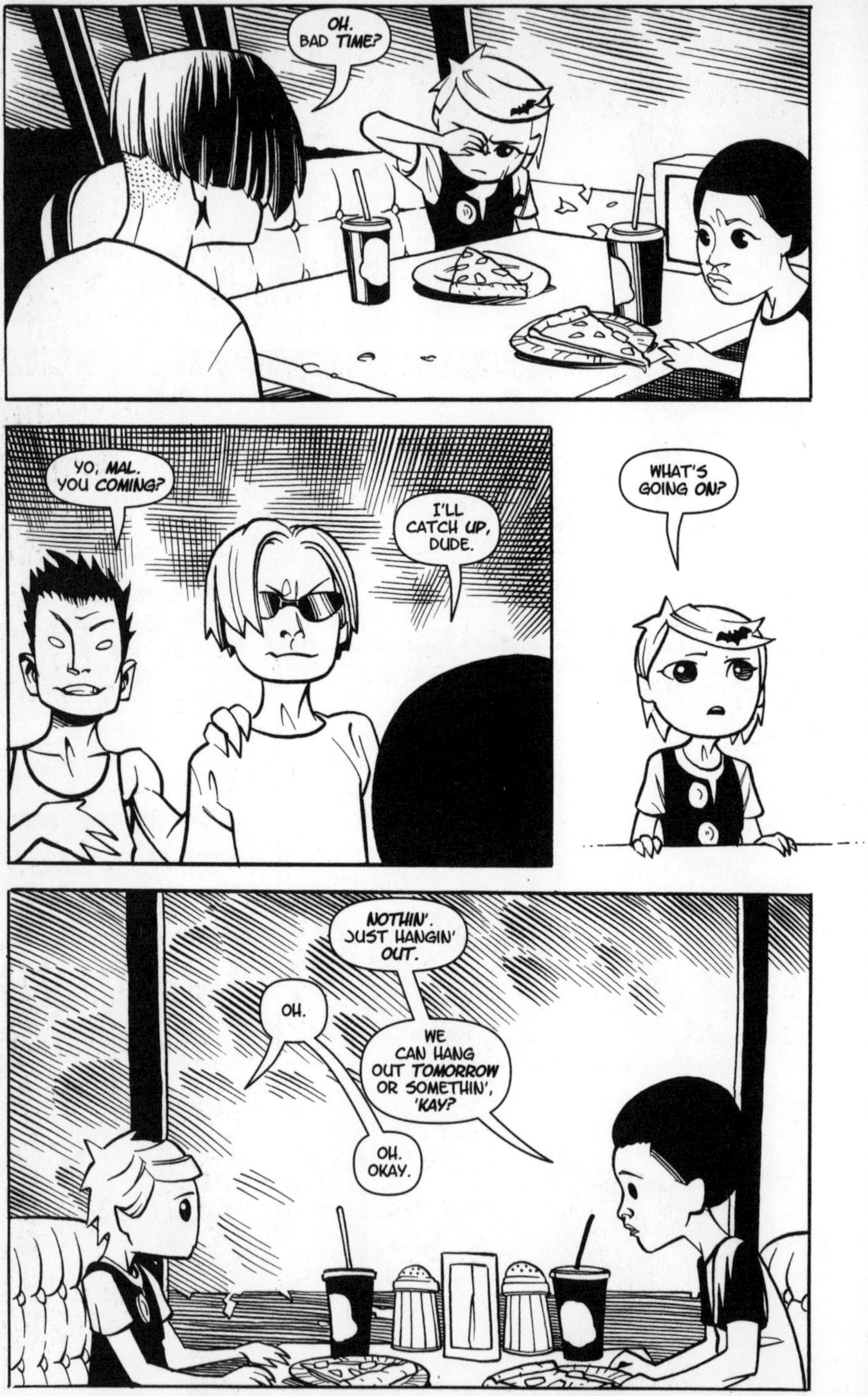
OH. BAD TIME?
YO, MAL. YOU COMING?
I'LL CATCH UP, DUDE.
WHAT'S GOING ON?
NOTHIN'. JUST HANGIN' OUT.
OH.
WE CAN HANG OUT TOMORROW OR SOMETHIN', 'KAY?
OH. OKAY.

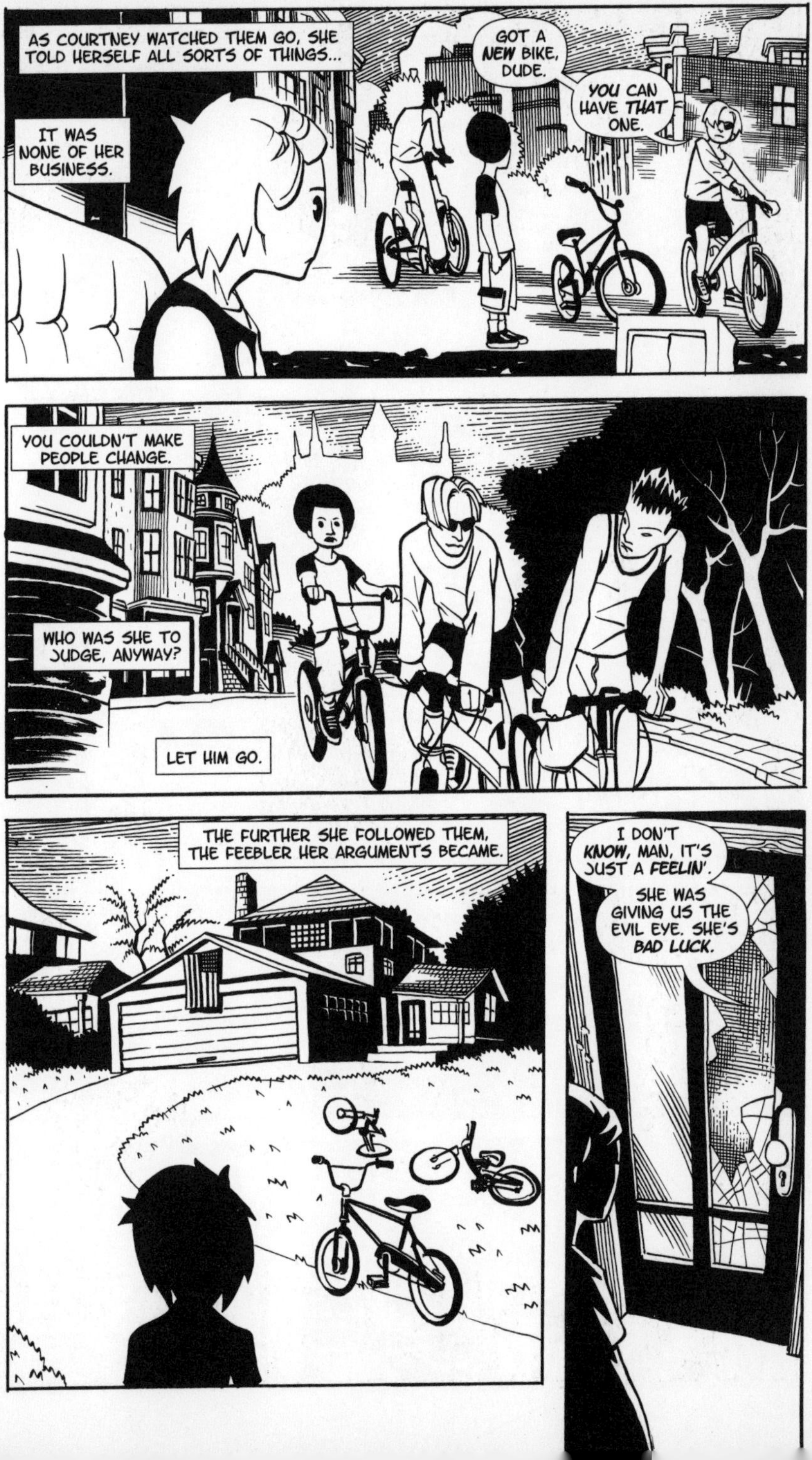
AS COURTNEY WATCHED THEM GO, SHE TOLD HERSELF ALL SORTS OF THINGS...
GOT A NEW BIKE, DUDE.
YOU CAN HAVE THAT ONE.
IT WAS NONE OF HER BUSINESS.
YOU COULDN'T MAKE PEOPLE CHANGE.
WHO WAS SHE TO JUDGE, ANYWAY?
LET HIM GO.
THE FURTHER SHE FOLLOWED THEM, THE FEEBLER HER ARGUMENTS BECAME.
I DON'T KNOW, MAN, IT'S JUST A FEELIN'.
SHE WAS GIVING US THE EVIL EYE. SHE'S BAD LUCK.

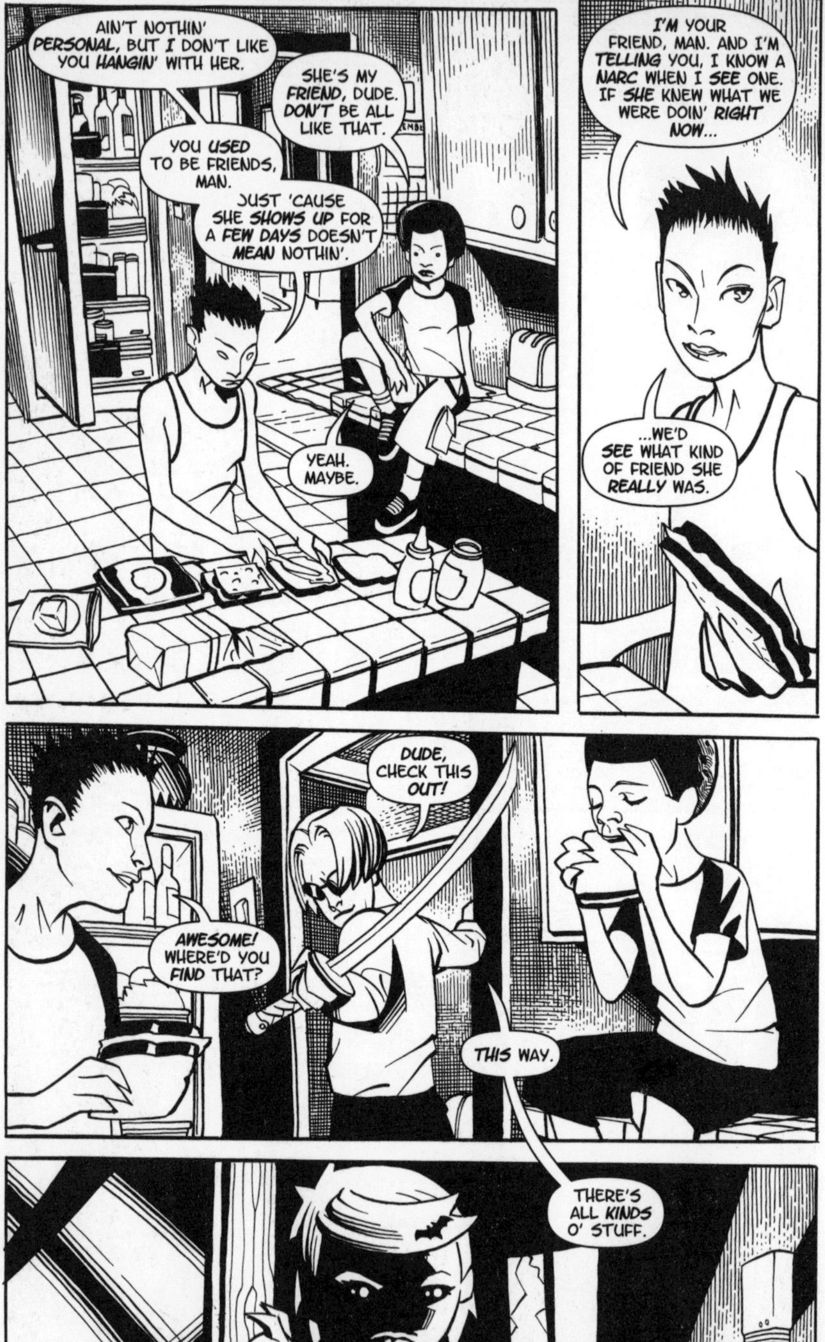
AIN'T NOTHIN' PERSONAL, BUT I DON'T LIKE YOU HANGIN' WITH HER.
SHE'S MY FRIEND, DUDE. DON'T BE ALL LIKE THAT.
YOU USED TO BE FRIENDS, MAN.
JUST 'CAUSE SHE SHOWS UP FOR A FEW DAYS DOESN'T MEAN NOTHIN'.
YEAH. MAYBE.
I'M YOUR FRIEND, MAN. AND I'M TELLING YOU, I KNOW A NARC WHEN I SEE ONE. IF SHE KNEW WHAT WE WERE DOIN' RIGHT NOW...
...WE'D SEE WHAT KIND OF FRIEND SHE REALLY WAS.
DUDE, CHECK THIS OUT!
AWESOME! WHERE'D YOU FIND THAT?
THIS WAY.
THERE'S ALL KINDS O' STUFF.

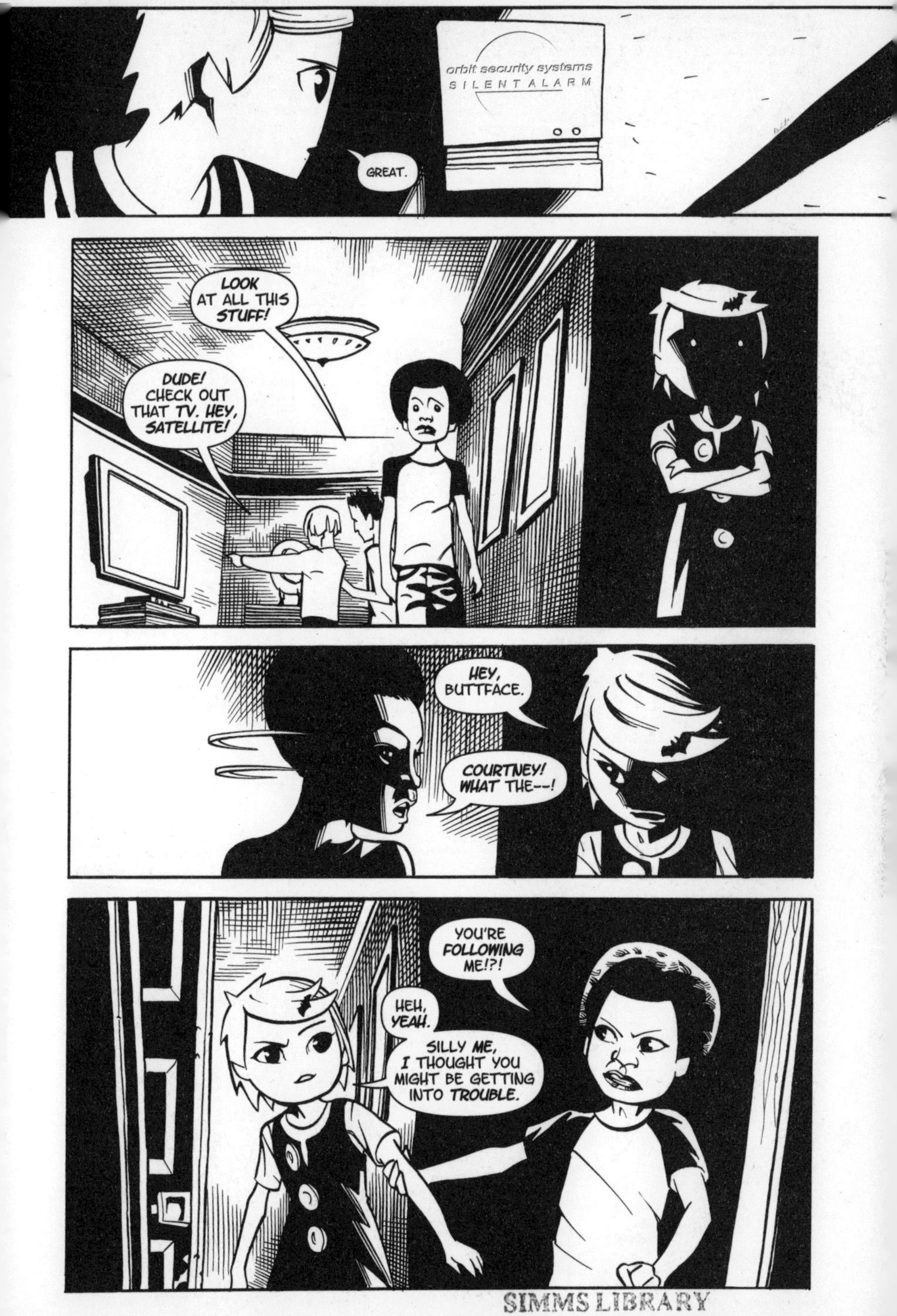
orbit security systems
SILENT ALARM
GREAT.
LOOK AT ALL THIS STUFF!
DUDE! CHECK OUT THAT TV. HEY, SATELLITE!
HEY, BUTTFACE.
COURTNEY! WHAT THE--!
YOU'RE FOLLOWING ME!?!
HEH, YEAH.
SILLY ME, I THOUGHT YOU MIGHT BE GETTING INTO TROUBLE.

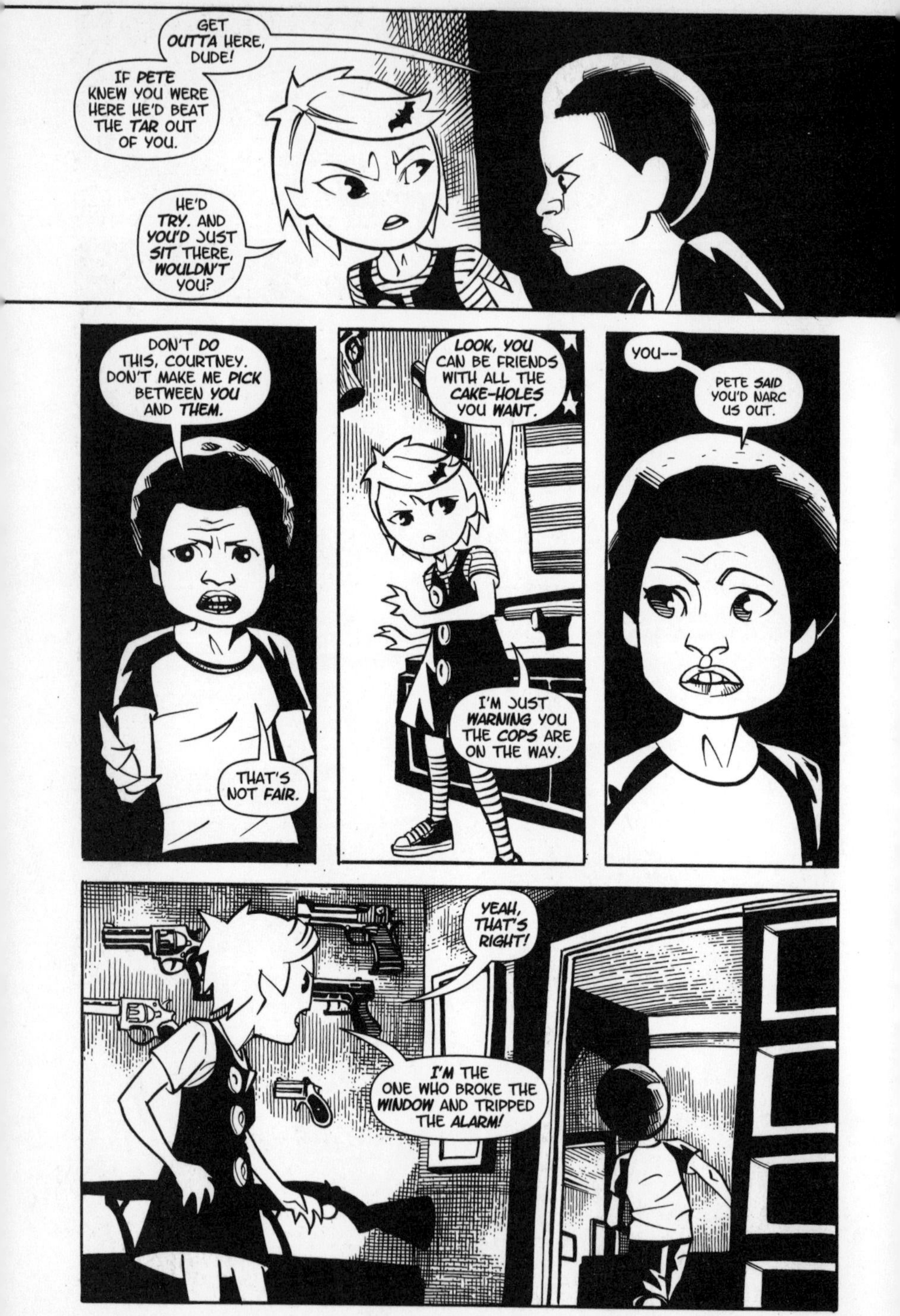
GET OUTTA HERE, DUDE!
IF PETE KNEW YOU WERE HERE HE'D BEAT THE TAR OUT OF YOU.
HE'D TRY. AND YOU'D JUST SIT THERE, WOULDN'T YOU?
DON'T DO THIS, COURTNEY. DON'T MAKE ME PICK BETWEEN YOU AND THEM.
THAT'S NOT FAIR.
LOOK, YOU CAN BE FRIENDS WITH ALL THE CAKE-HOLES YOU WANT.
I'M JUST WARNING YOU THE COPS ARE ON THE WAY.
YOU--
PETE SAID YOU'D NARC US OUT.
YEAH, THAT'S RIGHT!
I'M THE ONE WHO BROKE THE WINDOW AND TRIPPED THE ALARM!

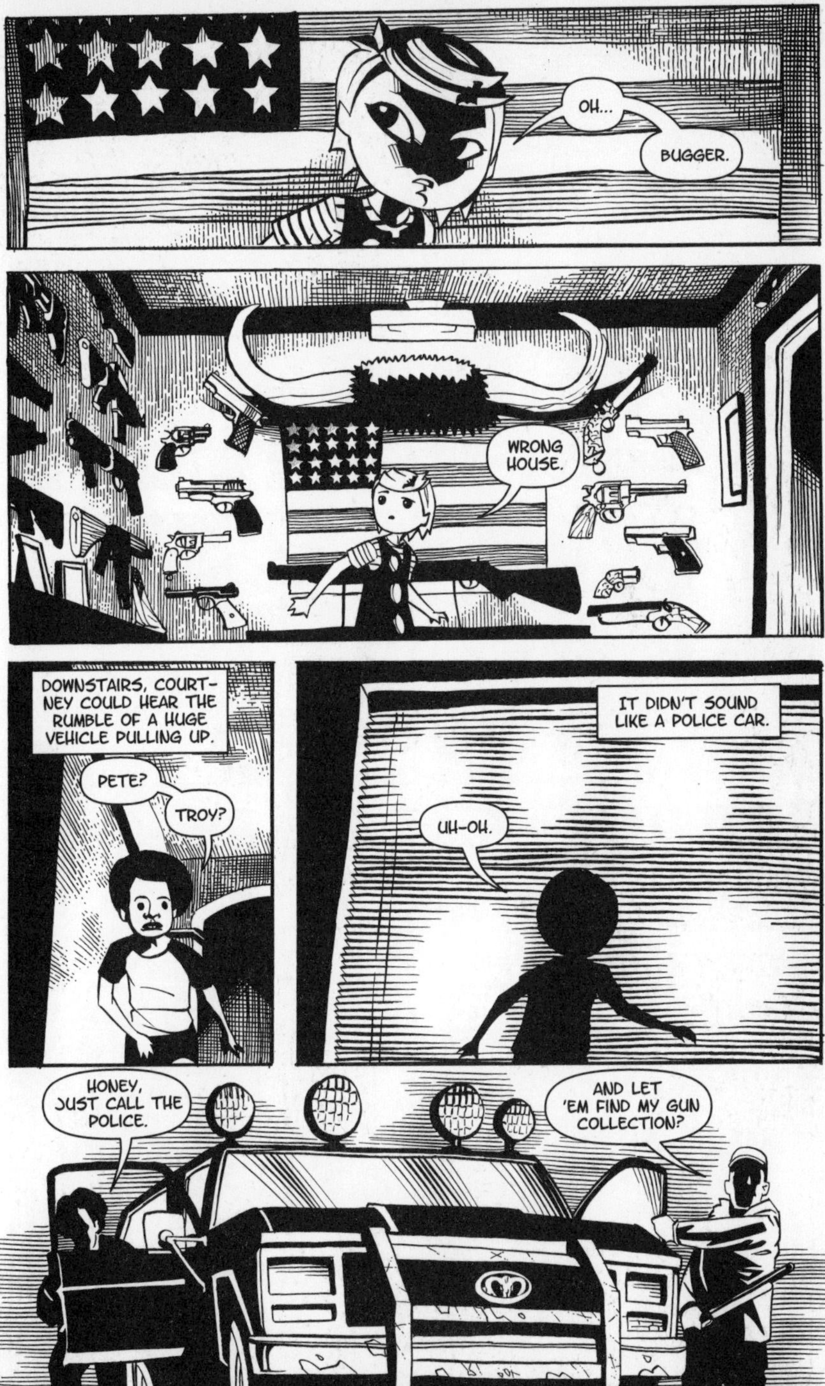
OH...
BUGGER.
WRONG HOUSE.
DOWNSTAIRS, COURTNEY COULD HEAR THE RUMBLE OF A HUGE VEHICLE PULLING UP.
PETE?
TROY?
IT DIDN'T SOUND LIKE A POLICE CAR.
UH-OH.
HONEY, JUST CALL THE POLICE.
AND LET 'EM FIND MY GUN COLLECTION?

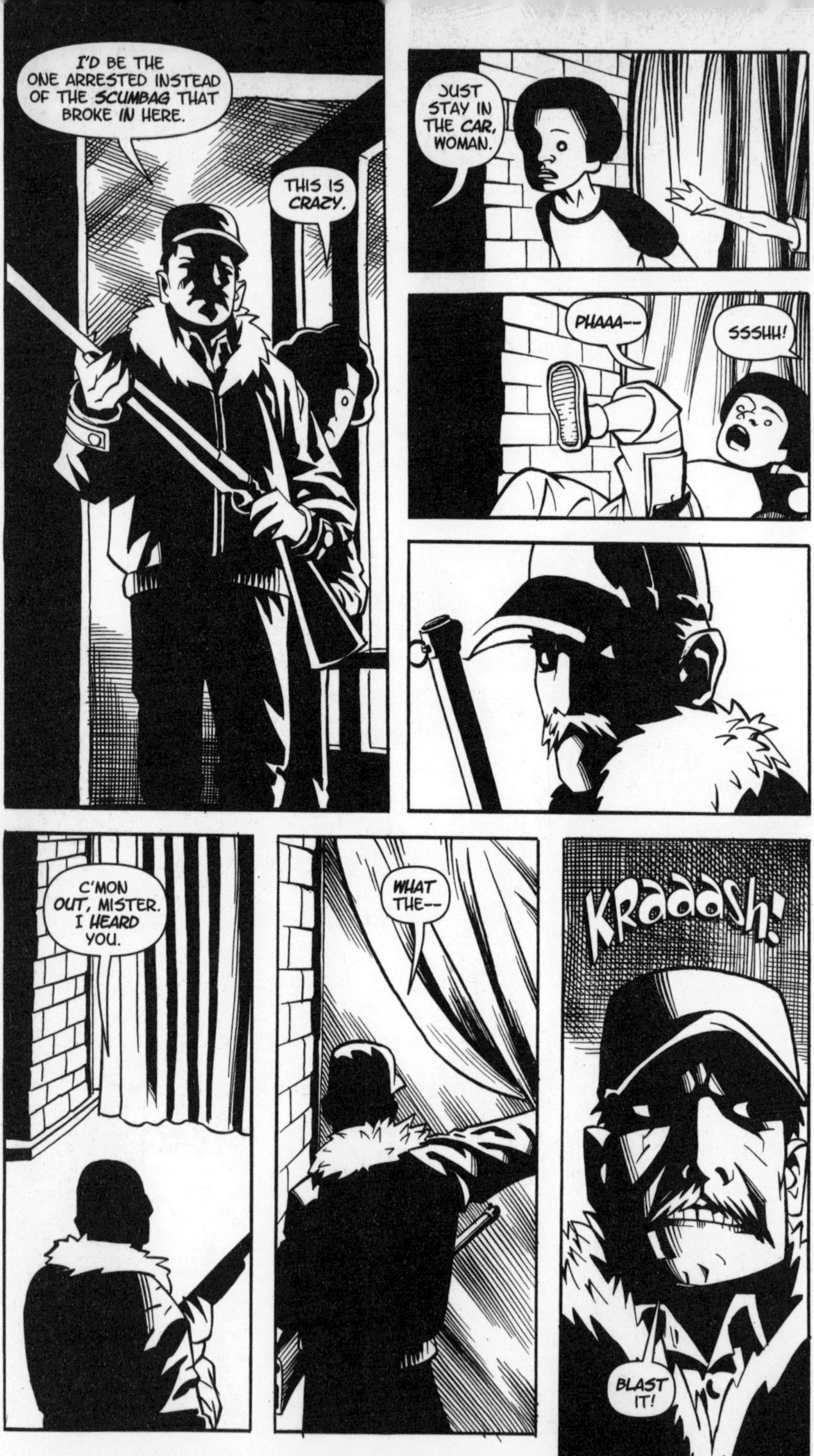
I'D BE THE ONE ARRESTED INSTEAD OF THE SCUMBAG THAT BROKE IN HERE.
THIS IS CRAZY.
JUST STAY IN THE CAR, WOMAN.
PHAAA--
SSSHH!
C'MON OUT, MISTER. I HEARD YOU.
WHAT THE--
KRAAASH!
BLAST IT!

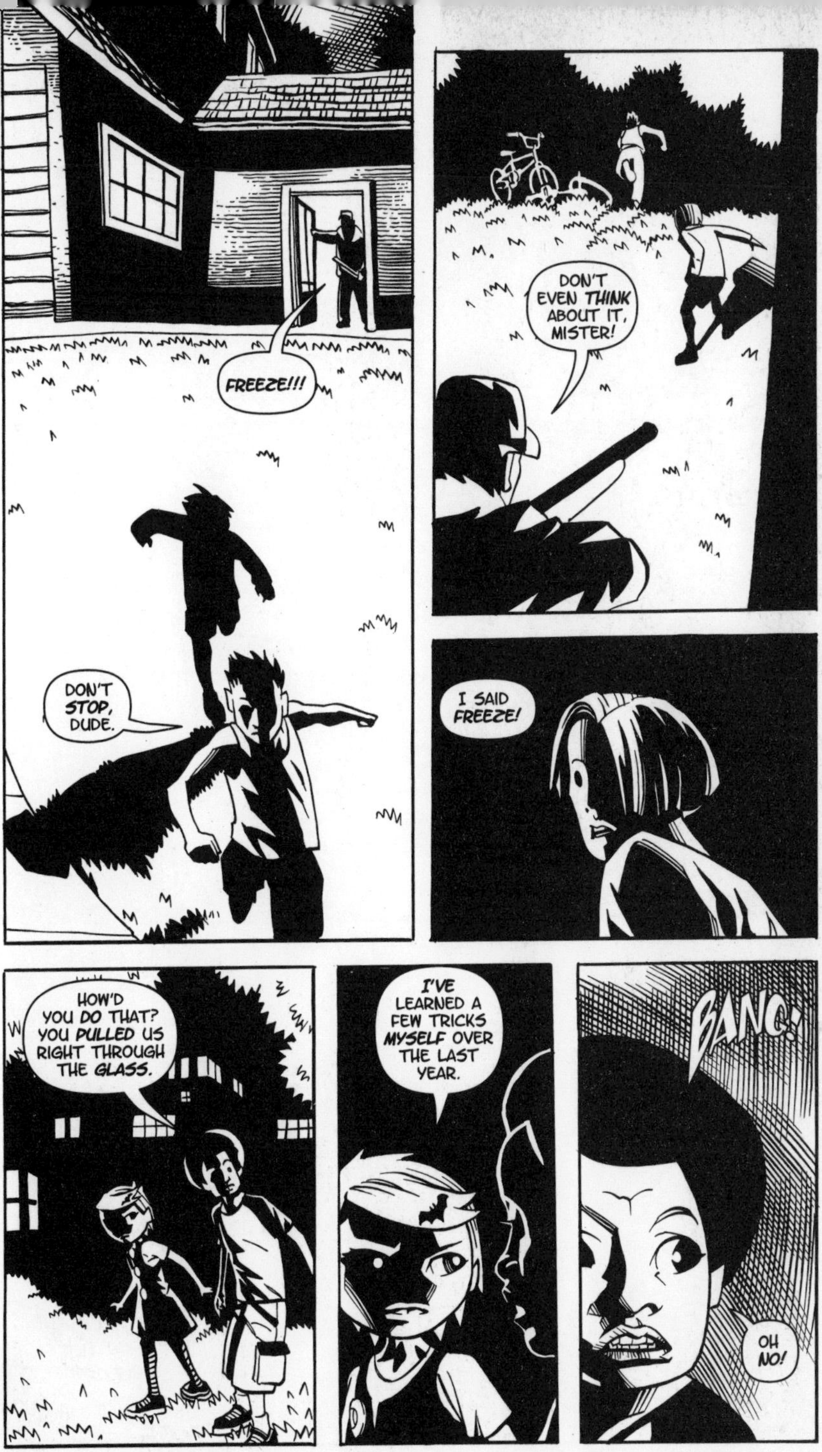
FREEZE!!!
DON'T STOP, DUDE.
DON'T EVEN THINK ABOUT IT, MISTER!
I SAID FREEZE!
HOW'D YOU DO THAT? YOU PULLED US RIGHT THROUGH THE GLASS.
I'VE LEARNED A FEW TRICKS MYSELF OVER THE LAST YEAR.
BANG!
OH NO!

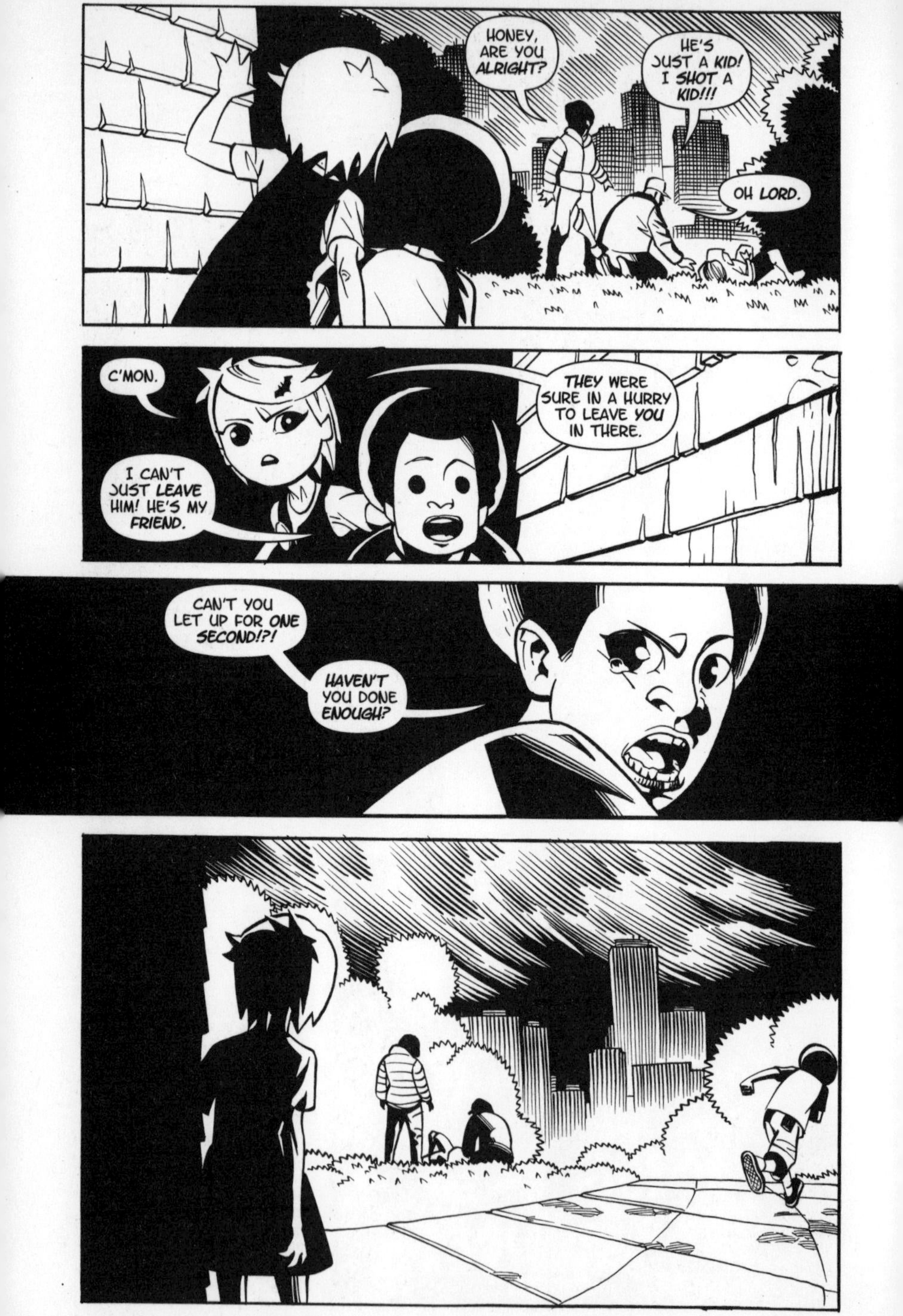
HONEY, ARE YOU ALRIGHT?
HE'S JUST A KID! I SHOT A KID!!!
OH LORD.
C'MON.
THEY WERE SURE IN A HURRY TO LEAVE YOU IN THERE.
I CAN'T JUST LEAVE HIM! HE'S MY FRIEND.
CAN'T YOU LET UP FOR ONE SECOND!?!
HAVEN'T YOU DONE ENOUGH?

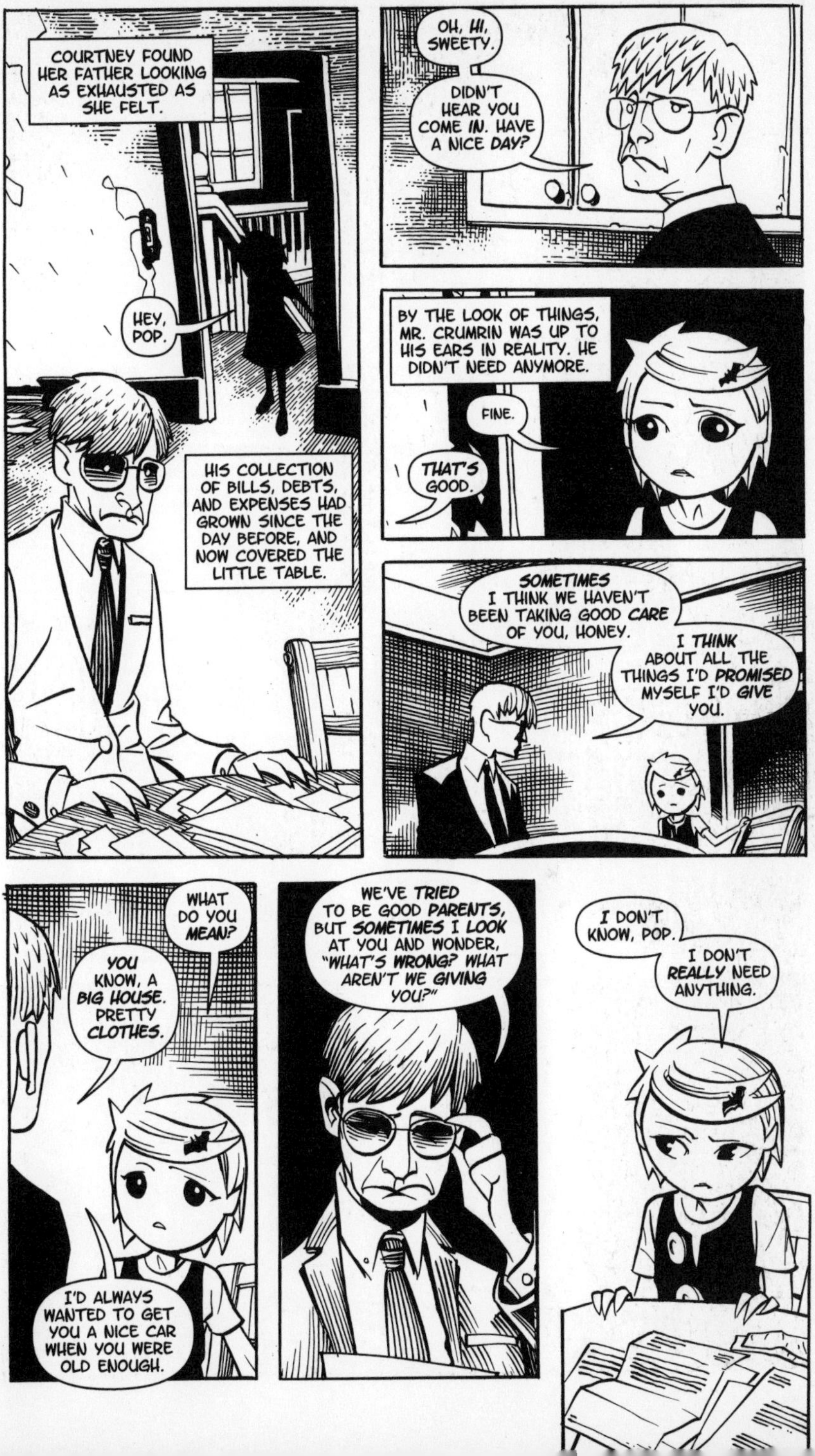

COURTNEY FOUND HER FATHER LOOKING AS EXHAUSTED AS SHE FELT.
HEY, POP.
HIS COLLECTION OF BILLS, DEBTS, AND EXPENSES HAD GROWN SINCE THE DAY BEFORE, AND NOW COVERED THE LITTLE TABLE.
OH, HI, SWEETY.
DIDN'T HEAR YOU COME IN. HAVE A NICE DAY?
BY THE LOOK OF THINGS, MR. CRUMRIN WAS UP TO HIS EARS IN REALITY. HE DIDN'T NEED ANYMORE.
FINE.
THAT'S GOOD.
SOMETIMES I THINK WE HAVEN'T BEEN TAKING GOOD CARE OF YOU, HONEY.
I THINK ABOUT ALL THE THINGS I'D PROMISED MYSELF I'D GIVE YOU.
WHAT DO YOU MEAN?
YOU KNOW, A BIG HOUSE. PRETTY CLOTHES.
I'D ALWAYS WANTED TO GET YOU A NICE CAR WHEN YOU WERE OLD ENOUGH.
WE'VE TRIED TO BE GOOD PARENTS, BUT SOMETIMES I LOOK AT YOU AND WONDER, "WHAT'S WRONG? WHAT AREN'T WE GIVING YOU?"
I DON'T KNOW, POP.
I DON'T REALLY NEED ANYTHING.

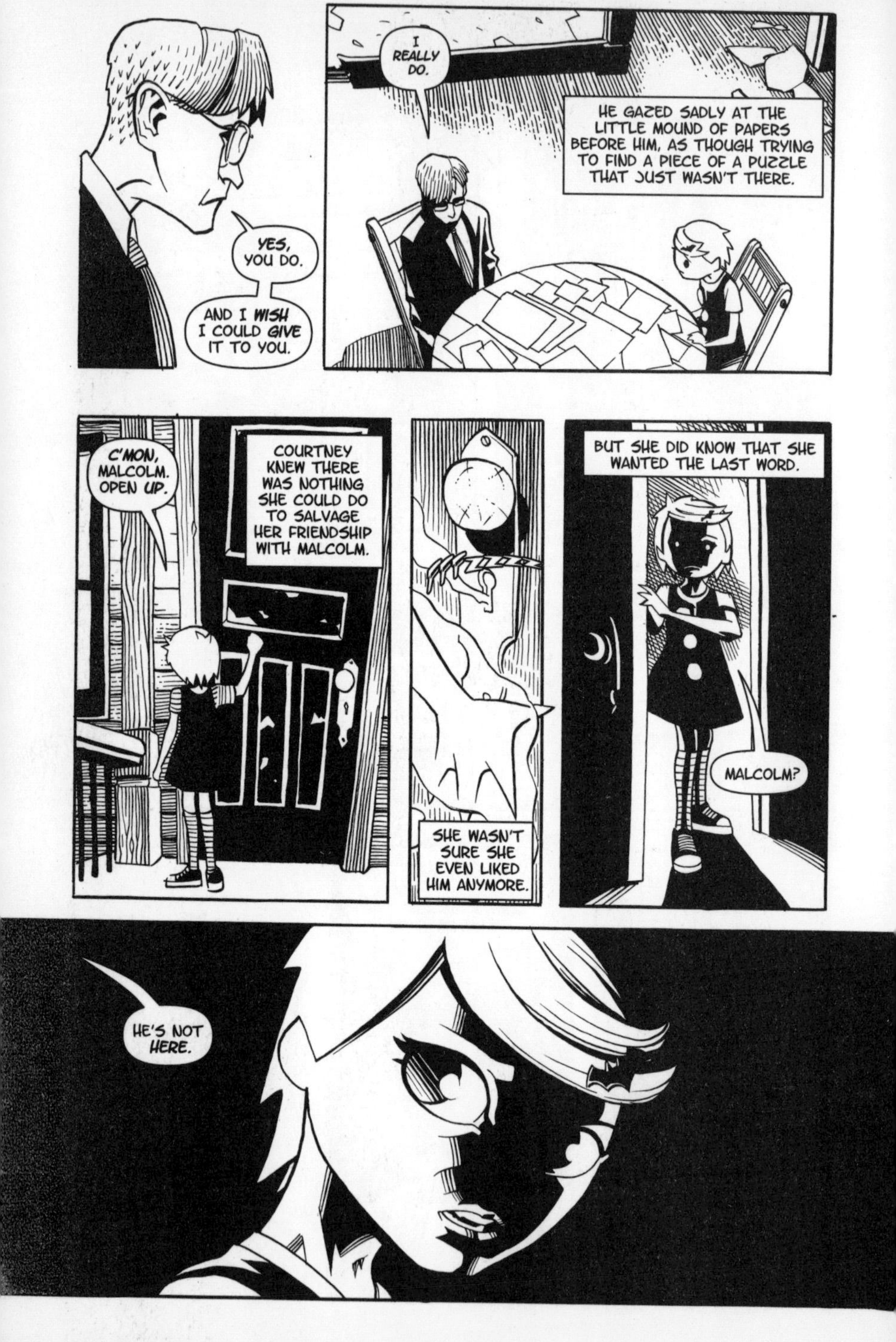
YES, YOU DO.
AND I WISH I COULD GIVE IT TO YOU.
I REALLY DO.
HE GAZED SADLY AT THE LITTLE MOUND OF PAPERS BEFORE HIM, AS THOUGH TRYING TO FIND A PIECE OF A PUZZLE THAT JUST WASN'T THERE.
C'MON, MALCOLM. OPEN UP.
COURTNEY KNEW THERE WAS NOTHING SHE COULD DO TO SALVAGE HER FRIENDSHIP WITH MALCOLM.
SHE WASN'T SURE SHE EVEN LIKED HIM ANYMORE.
BUT SHE DID KNOW THAT SHE WANTED THE LAST WORD.
MALCOLM?
HE'S NOT HERE.

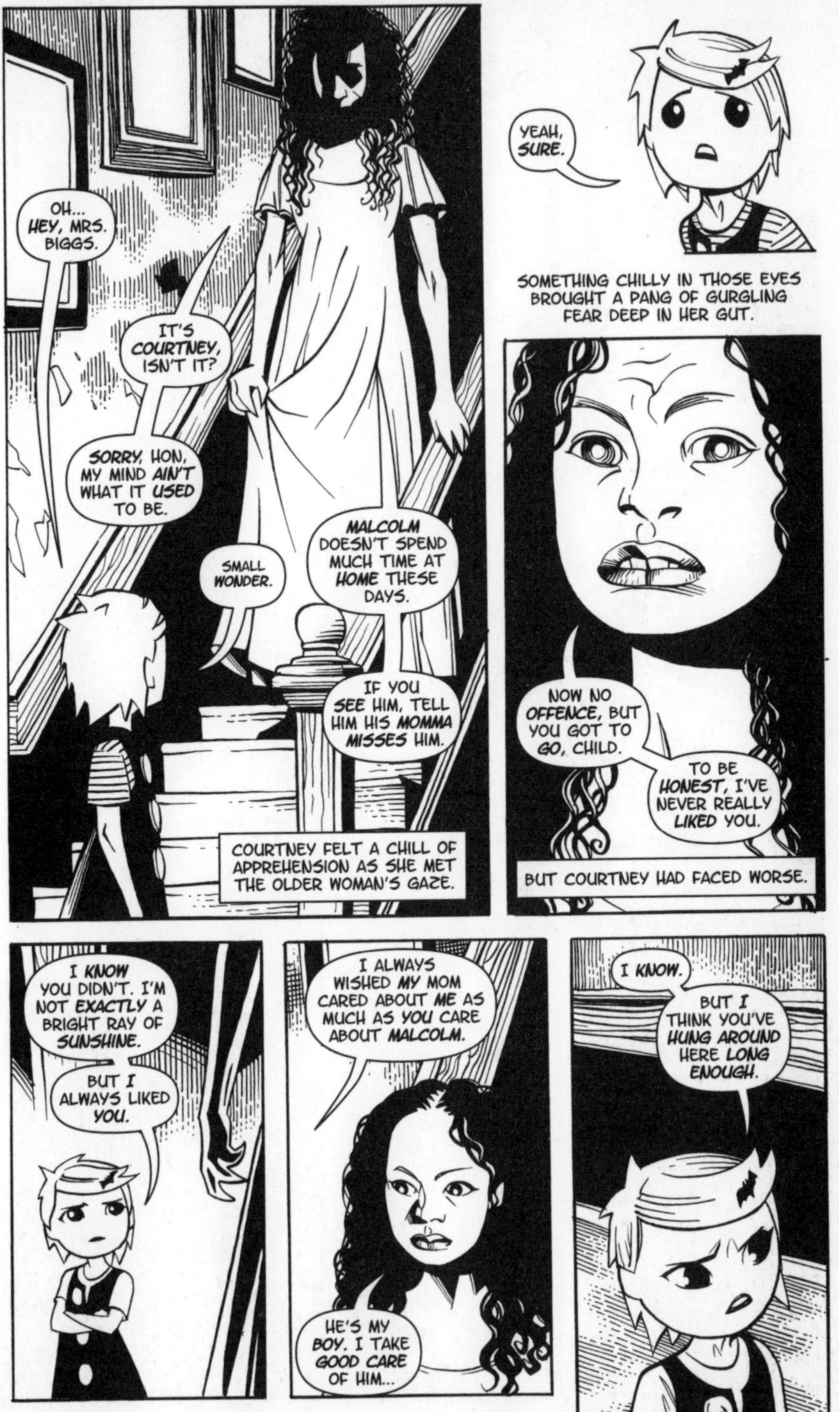

OH... HEY, MRS. BIGGS.
IT'S COURTNEY, ISN'T IT?
SORRY, HON, MY MIND AIN'T WHAT IT USED TO BE.
SMALL WONDER.
MALCOLM DOESN'T SPEND MUCH TIME AT HOME THESE DAYS.
IF YOU SEE HIM, TELL HIM HIS MOMMA MISSES HIM.
COURTNEY FELT A CHILL OF APPREHENSION AS SHE MET THE OLDER WOMAN'S GAZE.
YEAH, SURE.
SOMETHING CHILLY IN THOSE EYES BROUGHT A PANG OF GURGLING FEAR DEEP IN HER GUT.
NOW NO OFFENCE, BUT YOU GOT TO GO, CHILD.
TO BE HONEST, I'VE NEVER REALLY LIKED YOU.
BUT COURTNEY HAD FACED WORSE.
I KNOW YOU DIDN'T. I'M NOT EXACTLY A BRIGHT RAY OF SUNSHINE.
BUT I ALWAYS LIKED YOU.
I ALWAYS WISHED MY MOM CARED ABOUT ME AS MUCH AS YOU CARE ABOUT MALCOLM.
HE'S MY BOY. I TAKE GOOD CARE OF HIM...
I KNOW.
BUT I THINK YOU'VE HUNG AROUND HERE LONG ENOUGH.

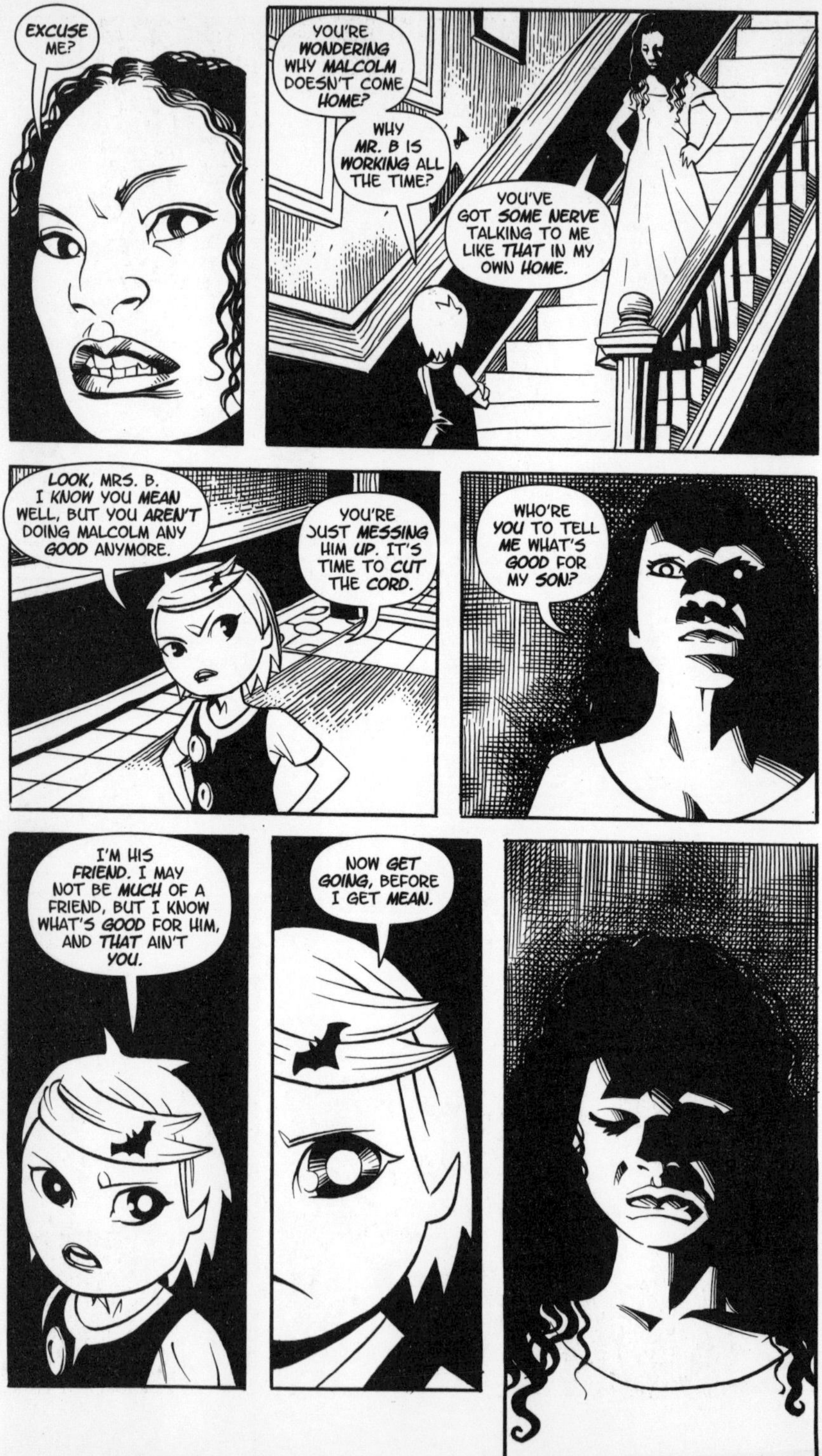
EXCUSE ME?
YOU'RE WONDERING WHY MALCOLM DOESN'T COME HOME?
WHY MR. B IS WORKING ALL THE TIME?
YOU'VE GOT SOME NERVE TALKING TO ME LIKE THAT IN MY OWN HOME.
LOOK, MRS. B. I KNOW YOU MEAN WELL, BUT YOU AREN'T DOING MALCOLM ANY GOOD ANYMORE.
YOU'RE JUST MESSING HIM UP. IT'S TIME TO CUT THE CORD.
WHO'RE YOU TO TELL ME WHAT'S GOOD FOR MY SON?
I'M HIS FRIEND. I MAY NOT BE MUCH OF A FRIEND, BUT I KNOW WHAT'S GOOD FOR HIM, AND THAT AIN'T YOU.
NOW GET GOING, BEFORE I GET MEAN.

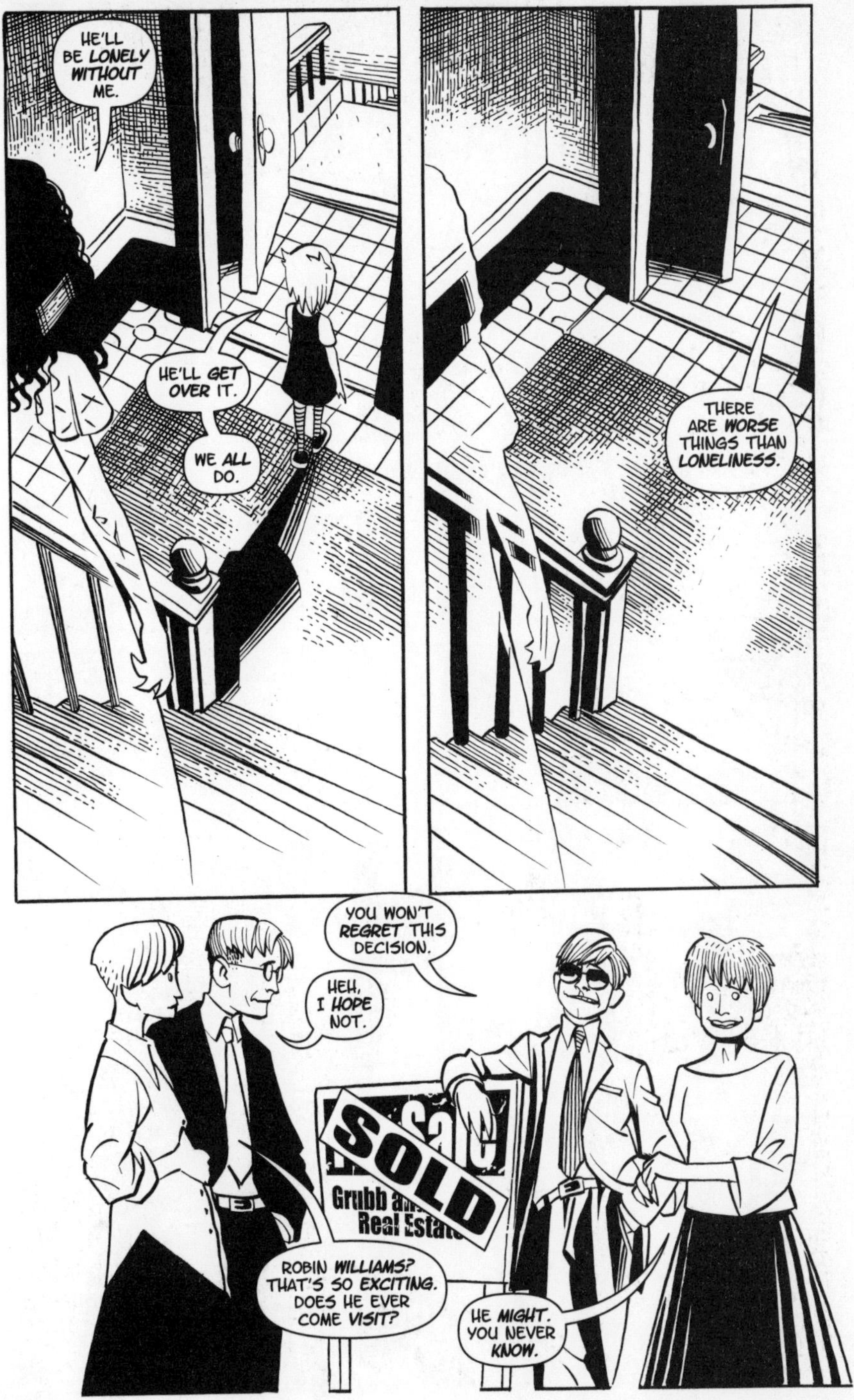
HE'LL BE LONELY WITHOUT ME.
HE'LL GET OVER IT.
WE ALL DO.
THERE ARE WORSE THINGS THAN LONELINESS.
YOU WON'T REGRET THIS DECISION.
HEH, I HOPE NOT.
SOLD
Grubb and Real Estate
ROBIN WILLIAMS? THAT'S SO EXCITING. DOES HE EVER COME VISIT?
HE MIGHT. YOU NEVER KNOW.

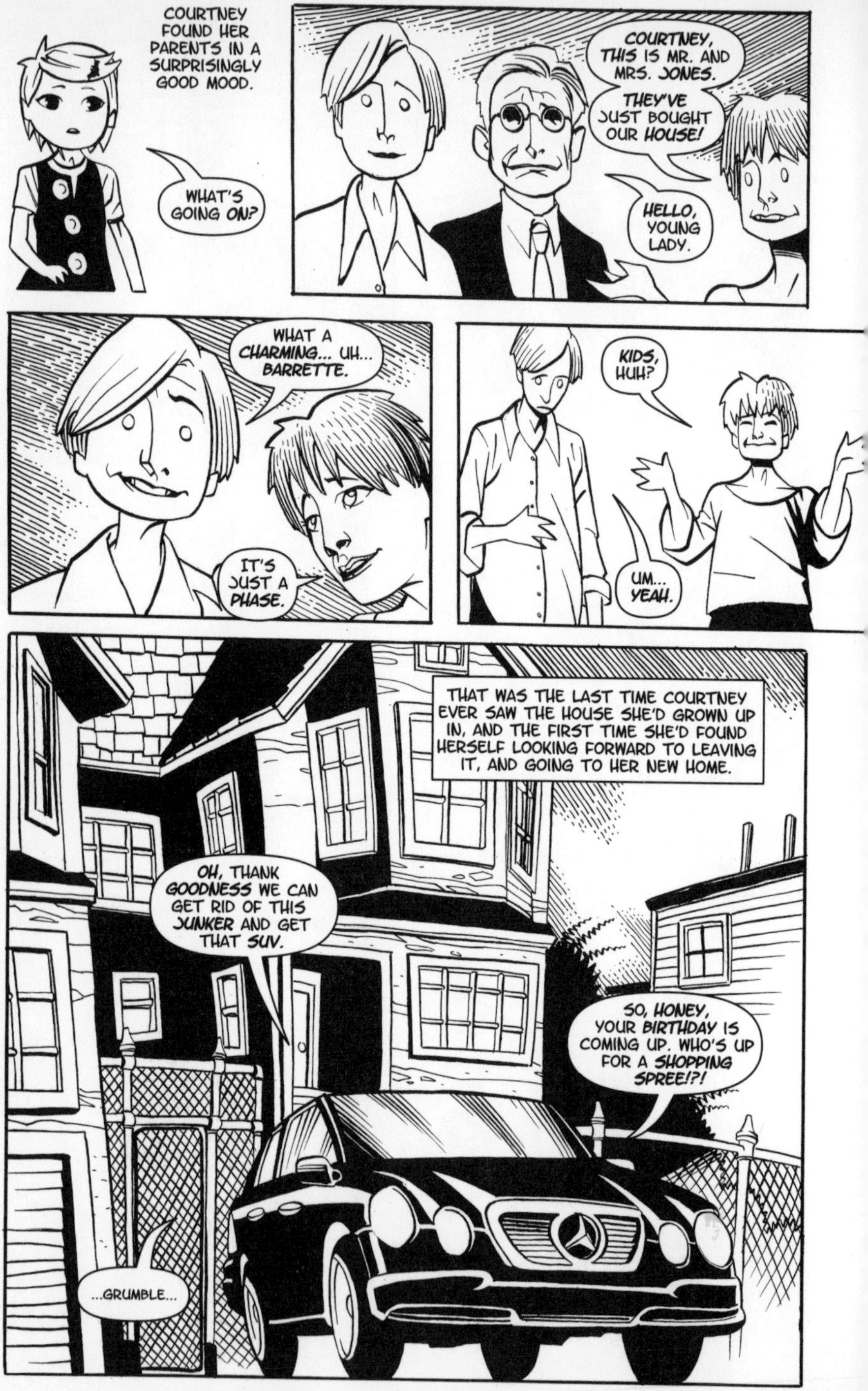
COURTNEY FOUND HER PARENTS IN A SURPRISINGLY GOOD MOOD.
WHAT'S GOING ON?
COURTNEY, THIS IS MR. AND MRS. JONES.
THEY'VE JUST BOUGHT OUR HOUSE!
HELLO, YOUNG LADY.
WHAT A CHARMING... UH... BARRETTE.
IT'S JUST A PHASE.
KIDS, HUH?
UM... YEAH.
THAT WAS THE LAST TIME COURTNEY EVER SAW THE HOUSE SHE'D GROWN UP IN, AND THE FIRST TIME SHE'D FOUND HERSELF LOOKING FORWARD TO LEAVING IT, AND GOING TO HER NEW HOME.
OH, THANK GOODNESS WE CAN GET RID OF THIS JUNKER AND GET THAT SUV.
SO, HONEY, YOUR BIRTHDAY IS COMING UP. WHO'S UP FOR A SHOPPING SPREE!?!
...GRUMBLE...

CHAPTER TWO

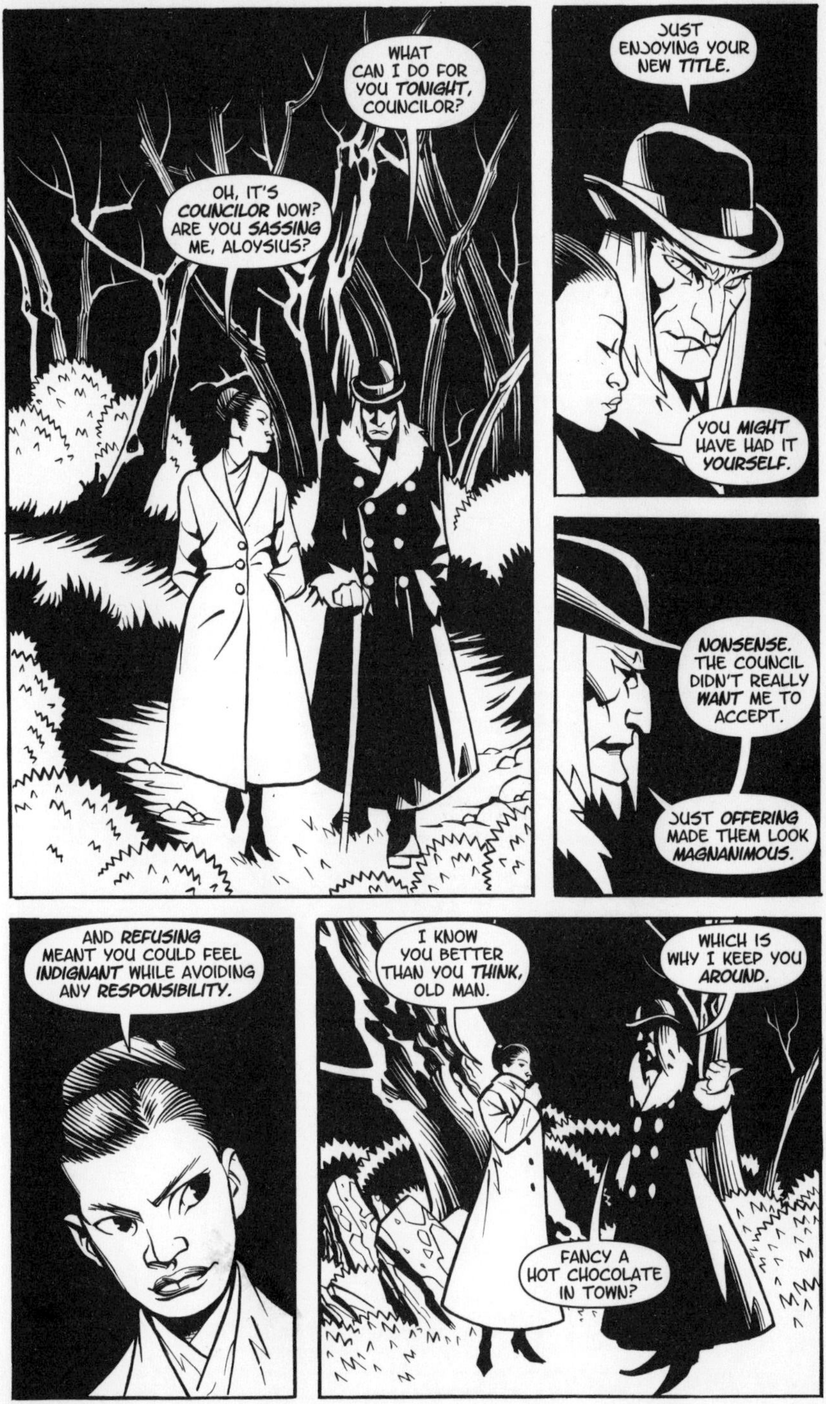
WHAT CAN I DO FOR YOU TONIGHT, COUNCILOR?
OH, IT'S COUNCILOR NOW? ARE YOU SASSING ME, ALOYSIUS?
JUST ENJOYING YOUR NEW TITLE.
YOU MIGHT HAVE HAD IT YOURSELF.
NONSENSE. THE COUNCIL DIDN'T REALLY WANT ME TO ACCEPT.
JUST OFFERING MADE THEM LOOK MAGNANIMOUS.
AND REFUSING MEANT YOU COULD FEEL INDIGNANT WHILE AVOIDING ANY RESPONSIBILITY.
I KNOW YOU BETTER THAN YOU THINK, OLD MAN.
WHICH IS WHY I KEEP YOU AROUND.
FANCY A HOT CHOCOLATE IN TOWN?

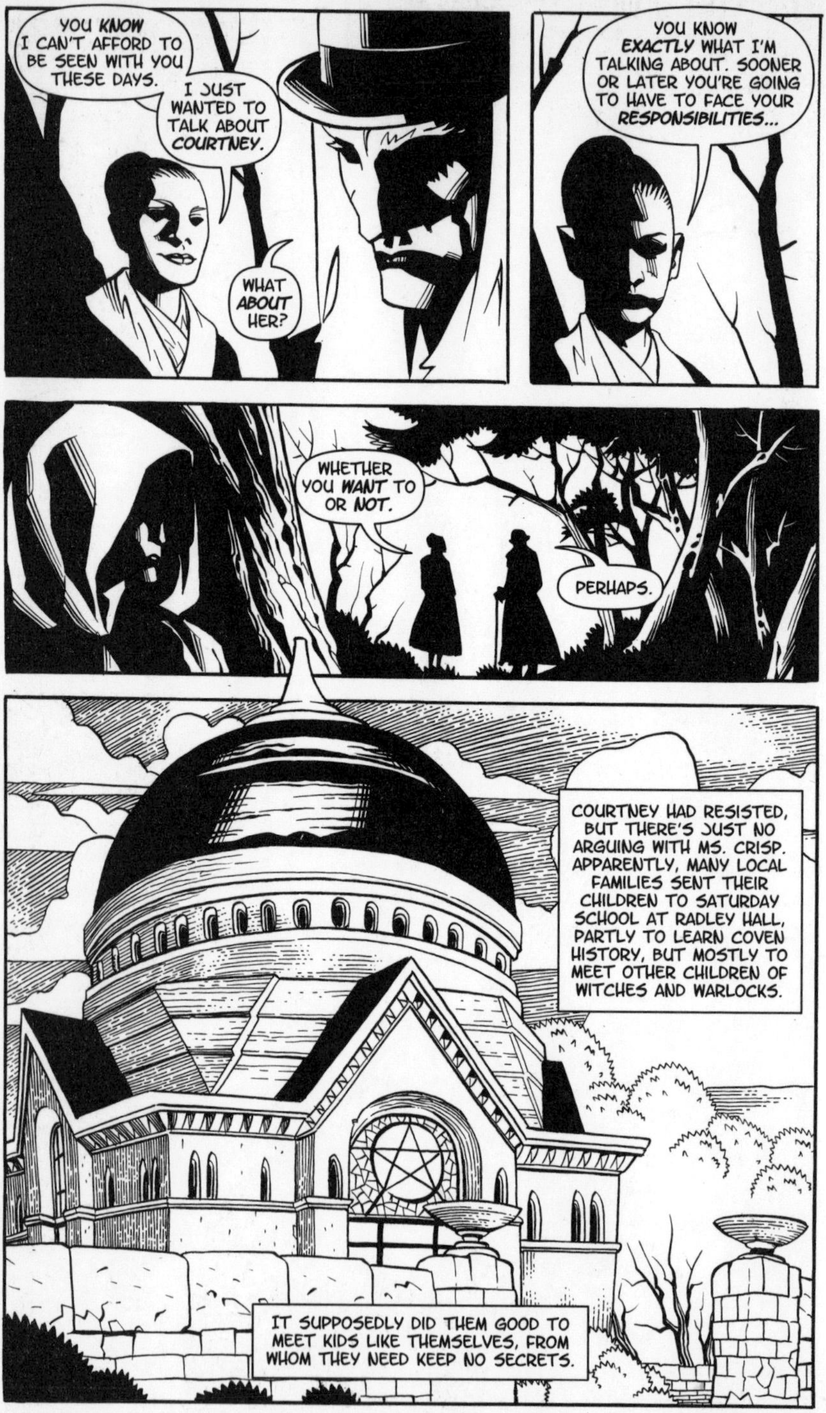
YOU KNOW I CAN'T AFFORD TO BE SEEN WITH YOU THESE DAYS.
I JUST WANTED TO TALK ABOUT COURTNEY.
WHAT ABOUT HER?
YOU KNOW EXACTLY WHAT I'M TALKING ABOUT. SOONER OR LATER YOU'RE GOING TO HAVE TO FACE YOUR RESPONSIBILITIES...
WHETHER YOU WANT TO OR NOT.
PERHAPS.
COURTNEY HAD RESISTED, BUT THERE'S JUST NO ARGUING WITH MS. CRISP. APPARENTLY, MANY LOCAL FAMILIES SENT THEIR CHILDREN TO SATURDAY SCHOOL AT RADLEY HALL, PARTLY TO LEARN COVEN HISTORY, BUT MOSTLY TO MEET OTHER CHILDREN OF WITCHES AND WARLOCKS.
IT SUPPOSEDLY DID THEM GOOD TO MEET KIDS LIKE THEMSELVES, FROM WHOM THEY NEED KEEP NO SECRETS.

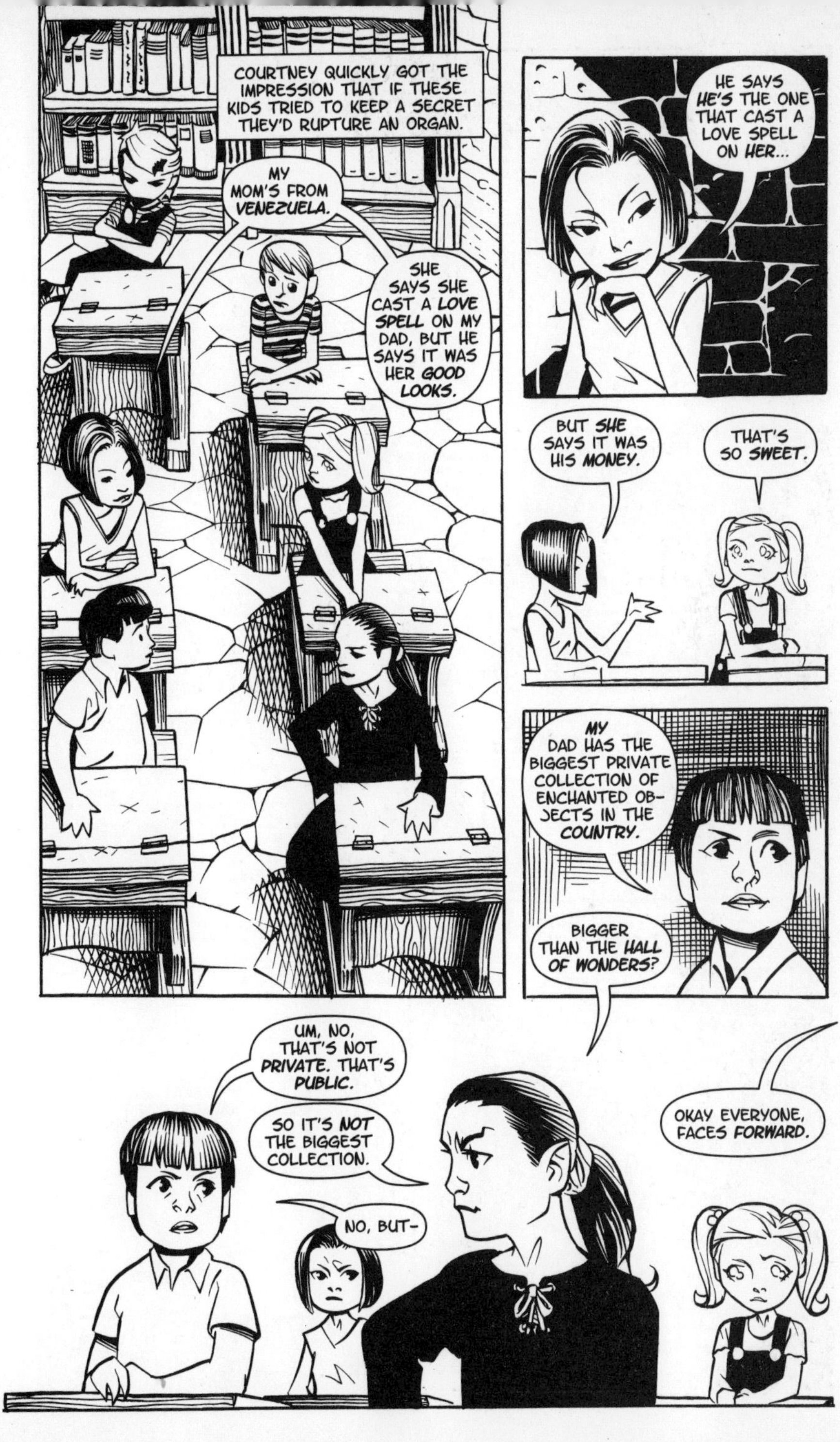
COURTNEY QUICKLY GOT THE IMPRESSION THAT IF THESE KIDS TRIED TO KEEP A SECRET THEY'D RUPTURE AN ORGAN.
MY MOM'S FROM VENEZUELA.
SHE SAYS SHE CAST A LOVE SPELL ON MY DAD, BUT HE SAYS IT WAS HER GOOD LOOKS.
HE SAYS HE'S THE ONE THAT CAST A LOVE SPELL ON HER...
BUT SHE SAYS IT WAS HIS MONEY.
THAT'S SO SWEET.
MY DAD HAS THE BIGGEST PRIVATE COLLECTION OF ENCHANTED OBJECTS IN THE COUNTRY.
BIGGER THAN THE HALL OF WONDERS?
UM, NO, THAT'S NOT PRIVATE. THAT'S PUBLIC.
SO IT'S NOT THE BIGGEST COLLECTION.
NO, BUT-
OKAY EVERYONE, FACES FORWARD.

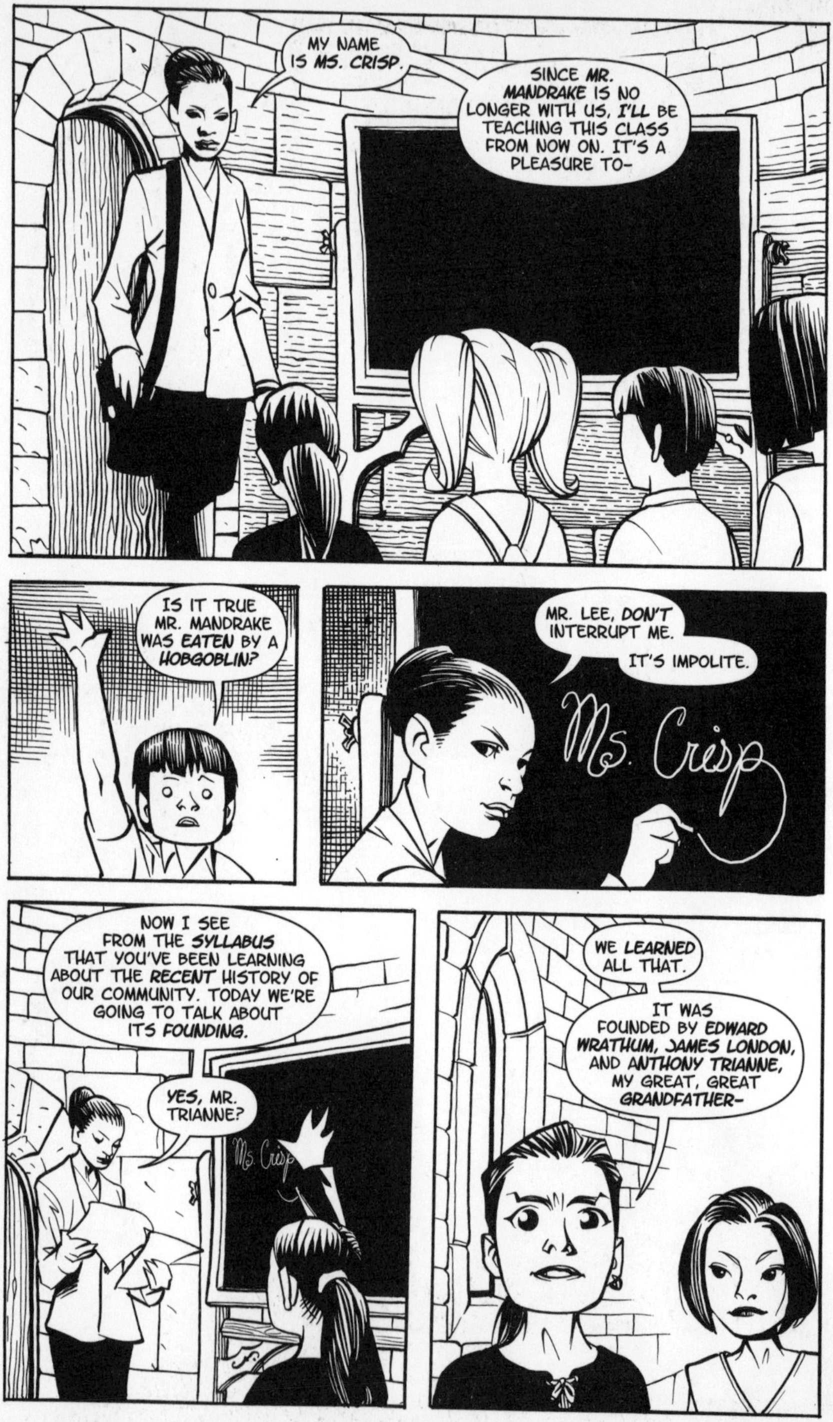
MY NAME IS MS. CRISP.
SINCE MR. MANDRAKE IS NO LONGER WITH US, I'LL BE TEACHING THIS CLASS FROM NOW ON. IT'S A PLEASURE TO-
IS IT TRUE MR. MANDRAKE WAS EATEN BY A HOBGOBLIN?
MR. LEE, DON'T INTERRUPT ME.
IT'S IMPOLITE.
Ms. Crisp
NOW I SEE FROM THE SYLLABUS THAT YOU'VE BEEN LEARNING ABOUT THE RECENT HISTORY OF OUR COMMUNITY. TODAY WE'RE GOING TO TALK ABOUT ITS FOUNDING.
YES, MR. TRIANNE?
Ms. Crisp
WE LEARNED ALL THAT.
IT WAS FOUNDED BY EDWARD WRATHUM, JAMES LONDON, AND ANTHONY TRIANNE, MY GREAT, GREAT GRANDFATHER-

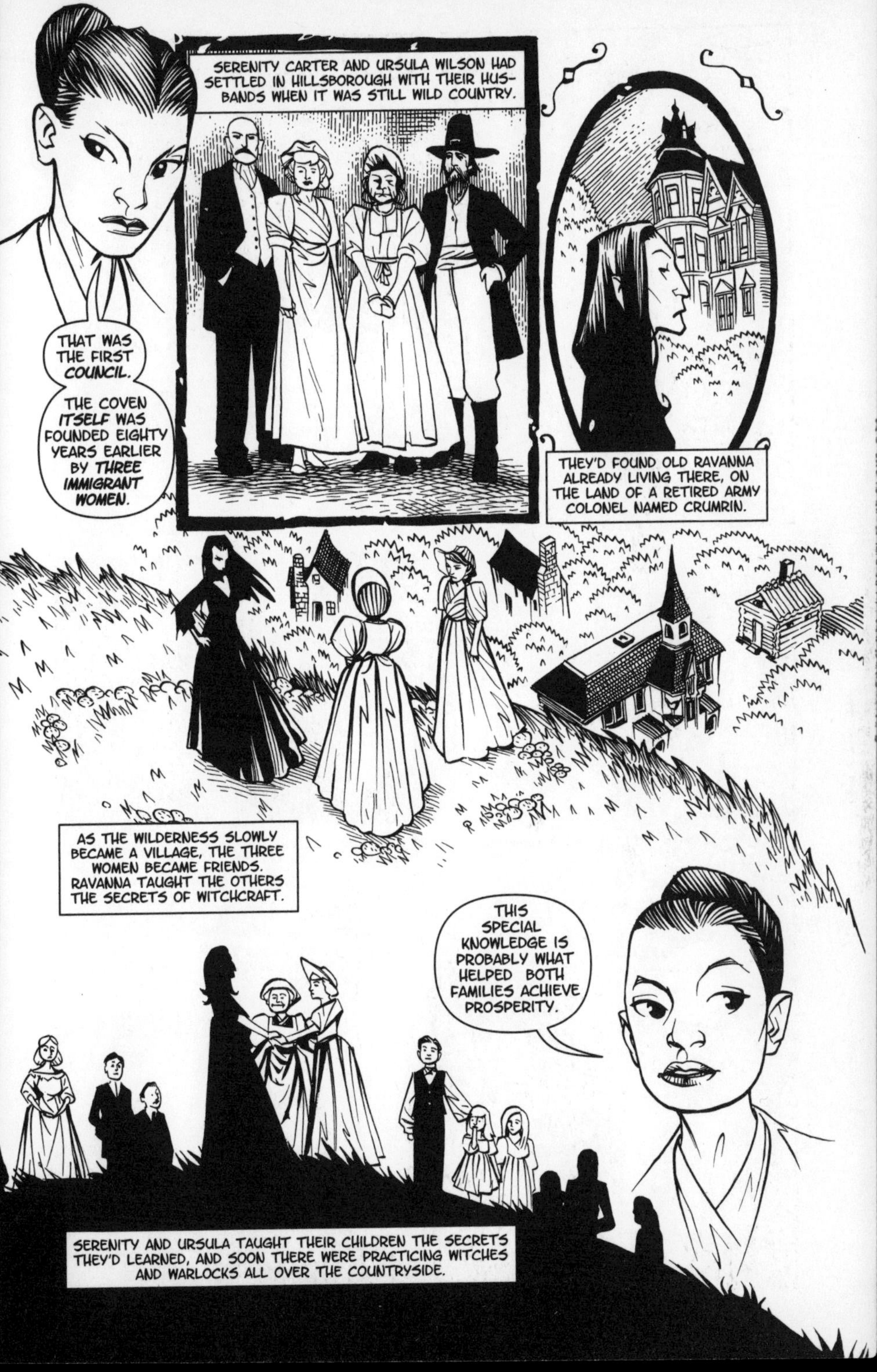
SERENITY CARTER AND URSULA WILSON HAD SETTLED IN HILLSBOROUGH WITH THEIR HUSBANDS WHEN IT WAS STILL WILD COUNTRY.
THAT WAS THE FIRST *COUNCIL.*
THE COVEN *ITSELF* WAS FOUNDED EIGHTY YEARS EARLIER BY *THREE IMMIGRANT WOMEN.*
THEY'D FOUND OLD RAVANNA ALREADY LIVING THERE, ON THE LAND OF A RETIRED ARMY COLONEL NAMED CRUMRIN.
AS THE WILDERNESS SLOWLY BECAME A VILLAGE, THE THREE WOMEN BECAME FRIENDS. RAVANNA TAUGHT THE OTHERS THE SECRETS OF WITCHCRAFT.
THIS SPECIAL KNOWLEDGE IS PROBABLY WHAT HELPED BOTH FAMILIES ACHIEVE PROSPERITY.
SERENITY AND URSULA TAUGHT THEIR CHILDREN THE SECRETS THEY'D LEARNED, AND SOON THERE WERE PRACTICING WITCHES AND WARLOCKS ALL OVER THE COUNTRYSIDE.

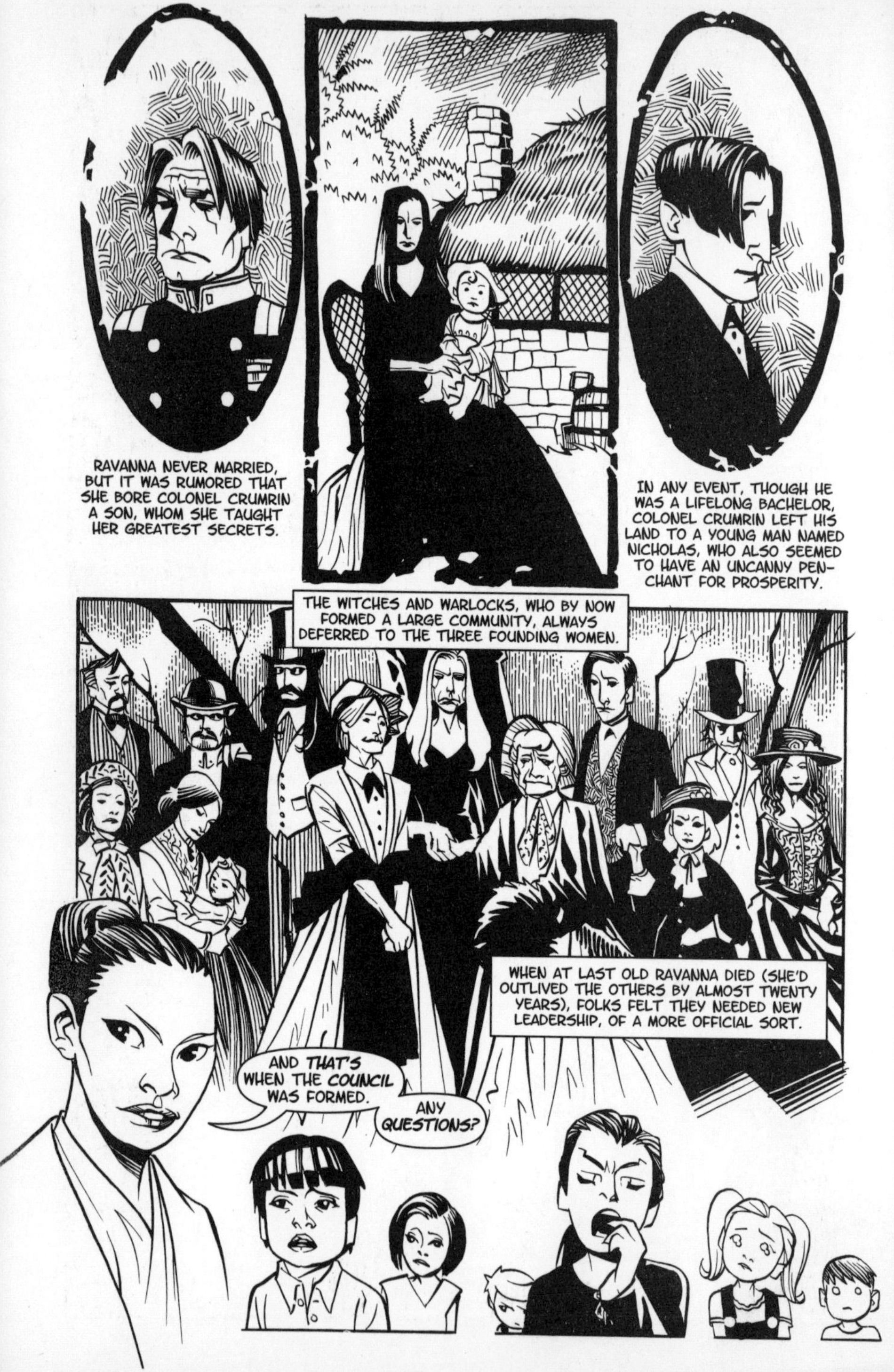

RAVANNA NEVER MARRIED, BUT IT WAS RUMORED THAT SHE BORE COLONEL CRUMRIN A SON, WHOM SHE TAUGHT HER GREATEST SECRETS.
IN ANY EVENT, THOUGH HE WAS A LIFELONG BACHELOR, COLONEL CRUMRIN LEFT HIS LAND TO A YOUNG MAN NAMED NICHOLAS, WHO ALSO SEEMED TO HAVE AN UNCANNY PENCHANT FOR PROSPERITY.
THE WITCHES AND WARLOCKS, WHO BY NOW FORMED A LARGE COMMUNITY, ALWAYS DEFERRED TO THE THREE FOUNDING WOMEN.
WHEN AT LAST OLD RAVANNA DIED (SHE'D OUTLIVED THE OTHERS BY ALMOST TWENTY YEARS), FOLKS FELT THEY NEEDED NEW LEADERSHIP, OF A MORE OFFICIAL SORT.
AND *THAT'S* WHEN THE *COUNCIL* WAS FORMED.
ANY *QUESTIONS?*

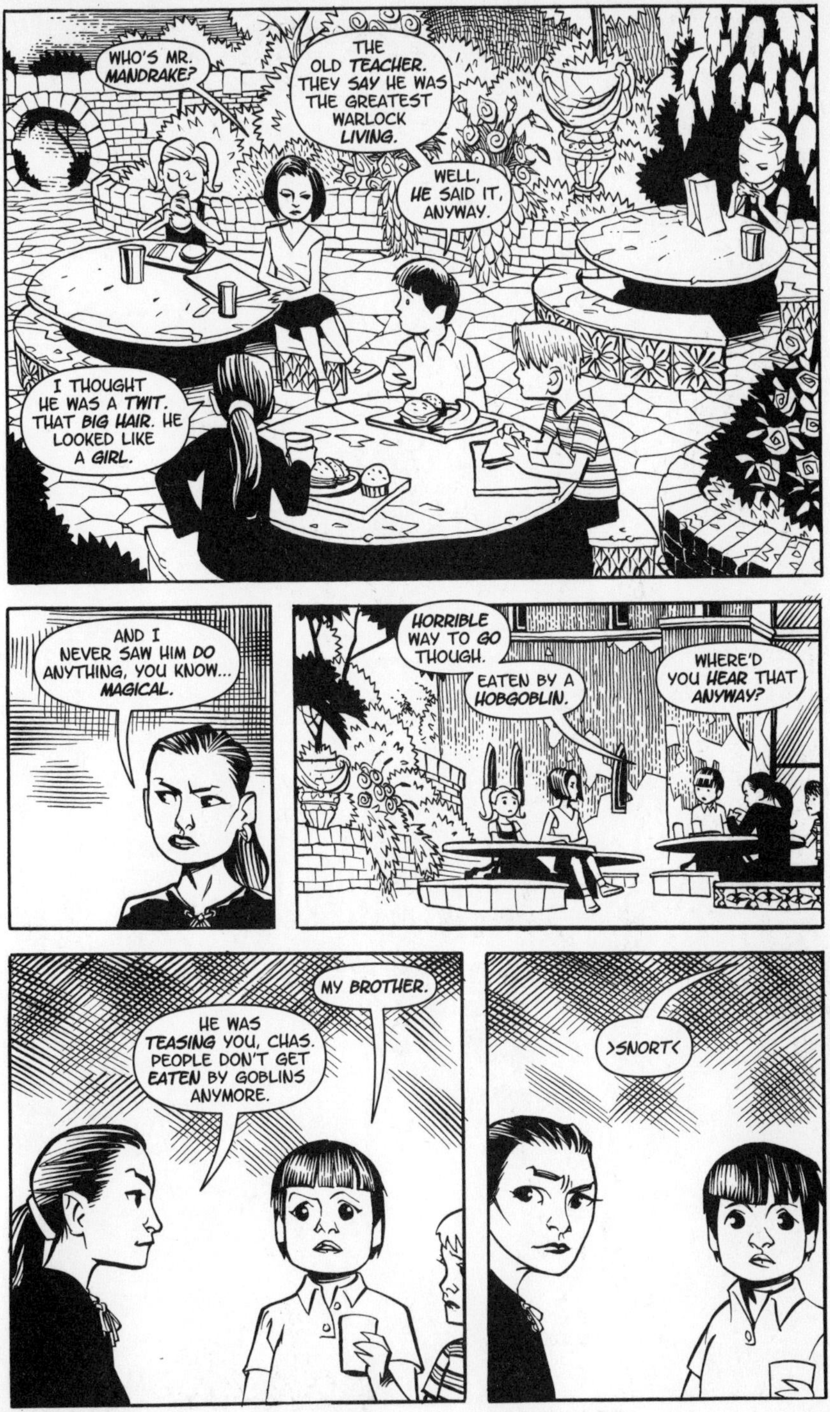
WHO'S MR. MANDRAKE?
THE OLD TEACHER. THEY SAY HE WAS THE GREATEST WARLOCK LIVING.
WELL, HE SAID IT, ANYWAY.
I THOUGHT HE WAS A TWIT. THAT BIG HAIR. HE LOOKED LIKE A GIRL.
AND I NEVER SAW HIM DO ANYTHING, YOU KNOW... MAGICAL.
HORRIBLE WAY TO GO THOUGH.
EATEN BY A HOBGOBLIN.
WHERE'D YOU HEAR THAT ANYWAY?
MY BROTHER.
HE WAS TEASING YOU, CHAS. PEOPLE DON'T GET EATEN BY GOBLINS ANYMORE.
>SNORT<

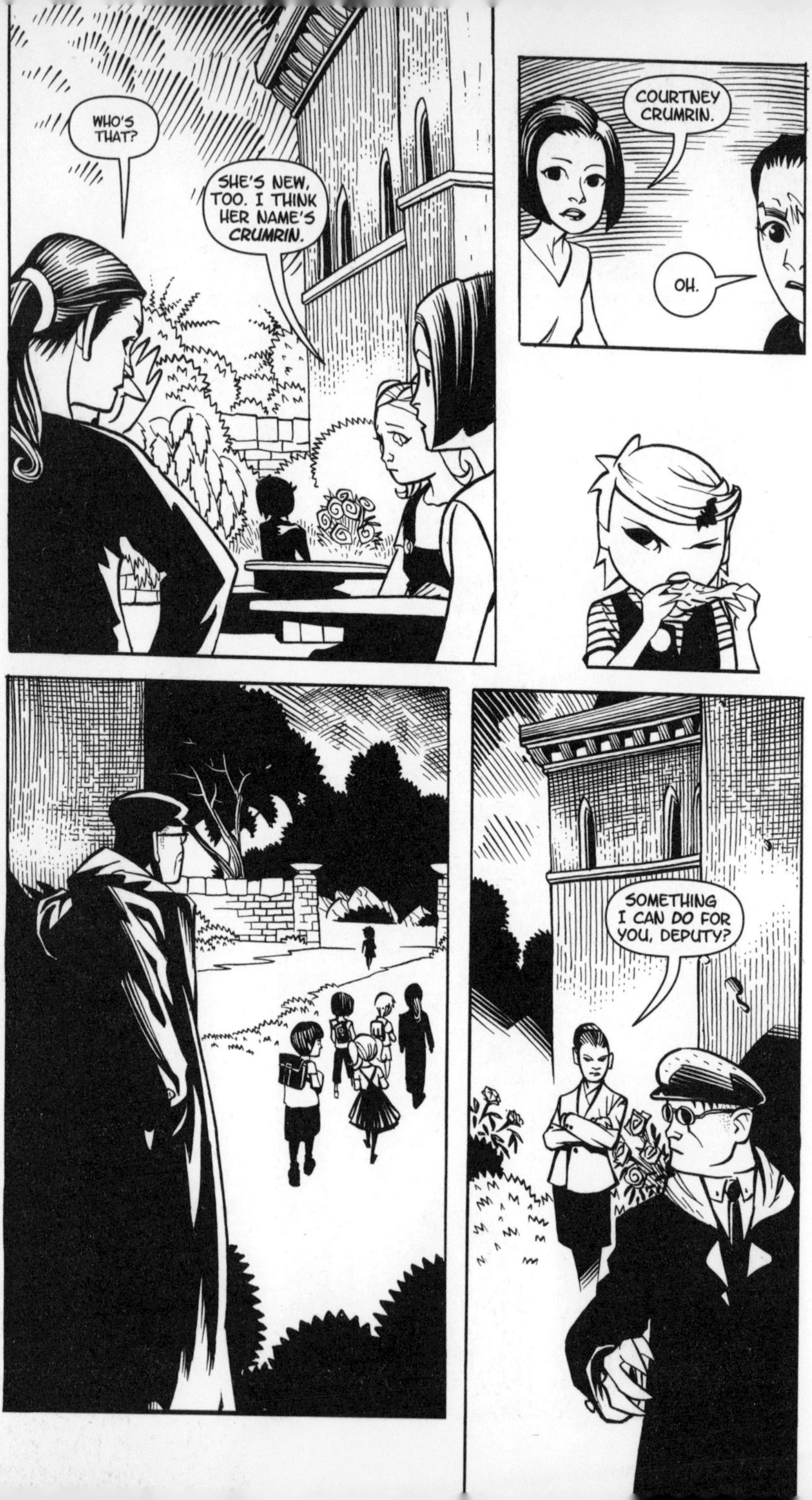
WHO'S THAT?
SHE'S NEW, TOO. I THINK HER NAME'S CRUMRIN.
COURTNEY CRUMRIN.
OH.
SOMETHING I CAN DO FOR YOU, DEPUTY?

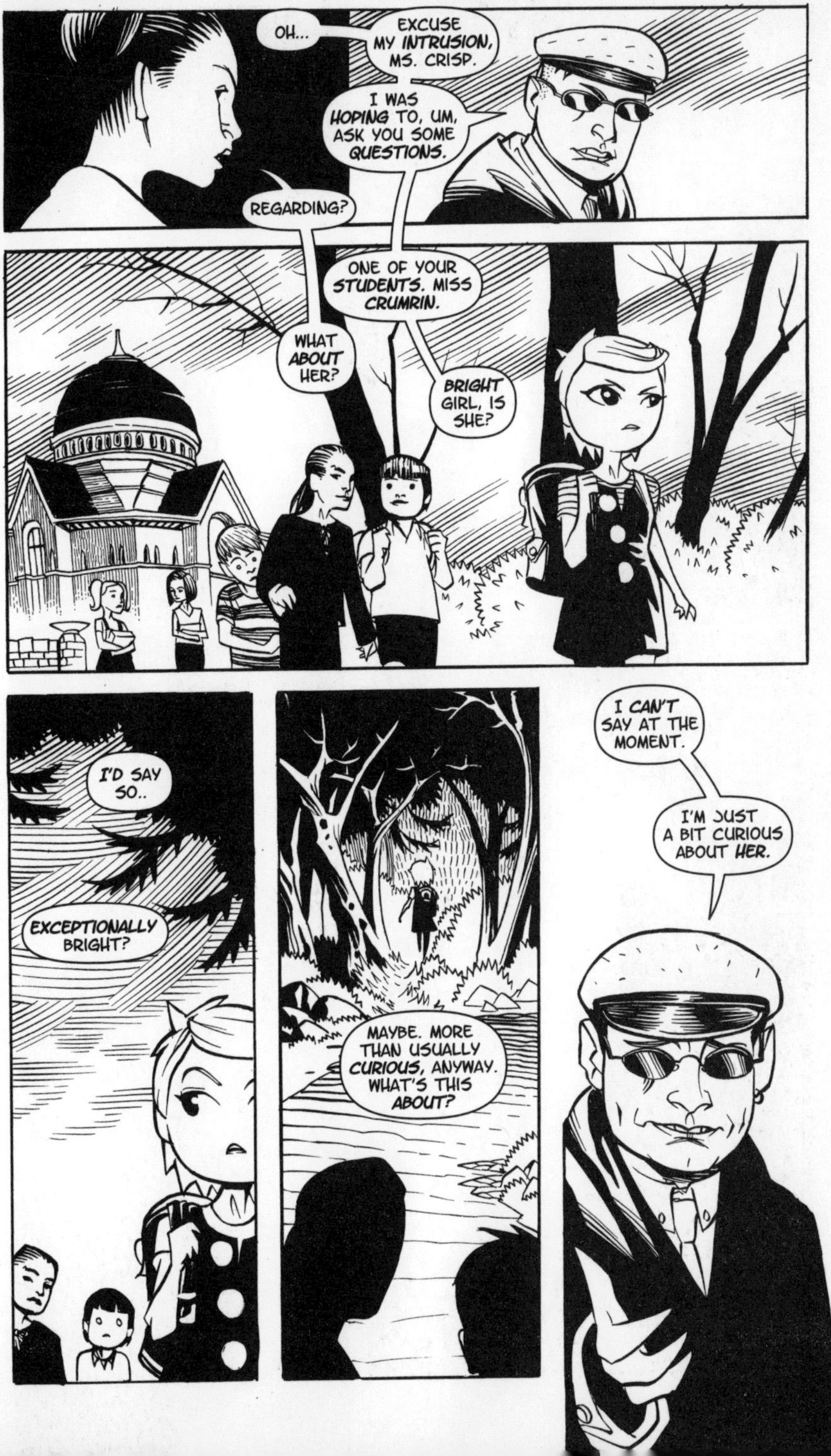
OH...
EXCUSE MY INTRUSION, MS. CRISP.
I WAS HOPING TO, UM, ASK YOU SOME QUESTIONS.
REGARDING?
ONE OF YOUR STUDENTS. MISS CRUMRIN.
WHAT ABOUT HER?
BRIGHT GIRL, IS SHE?
I'D SAY SO..
EXCEPTIONALLY BRIGHT?
MAYBE. MORE THAN USUALLY CURIOUS, ANYWAY. WHAT'S THIS ABOUT?
I CAN'T SAY AT THE MOMENT.
I'M JUST A BIT CURIOUS ABOUT HER.

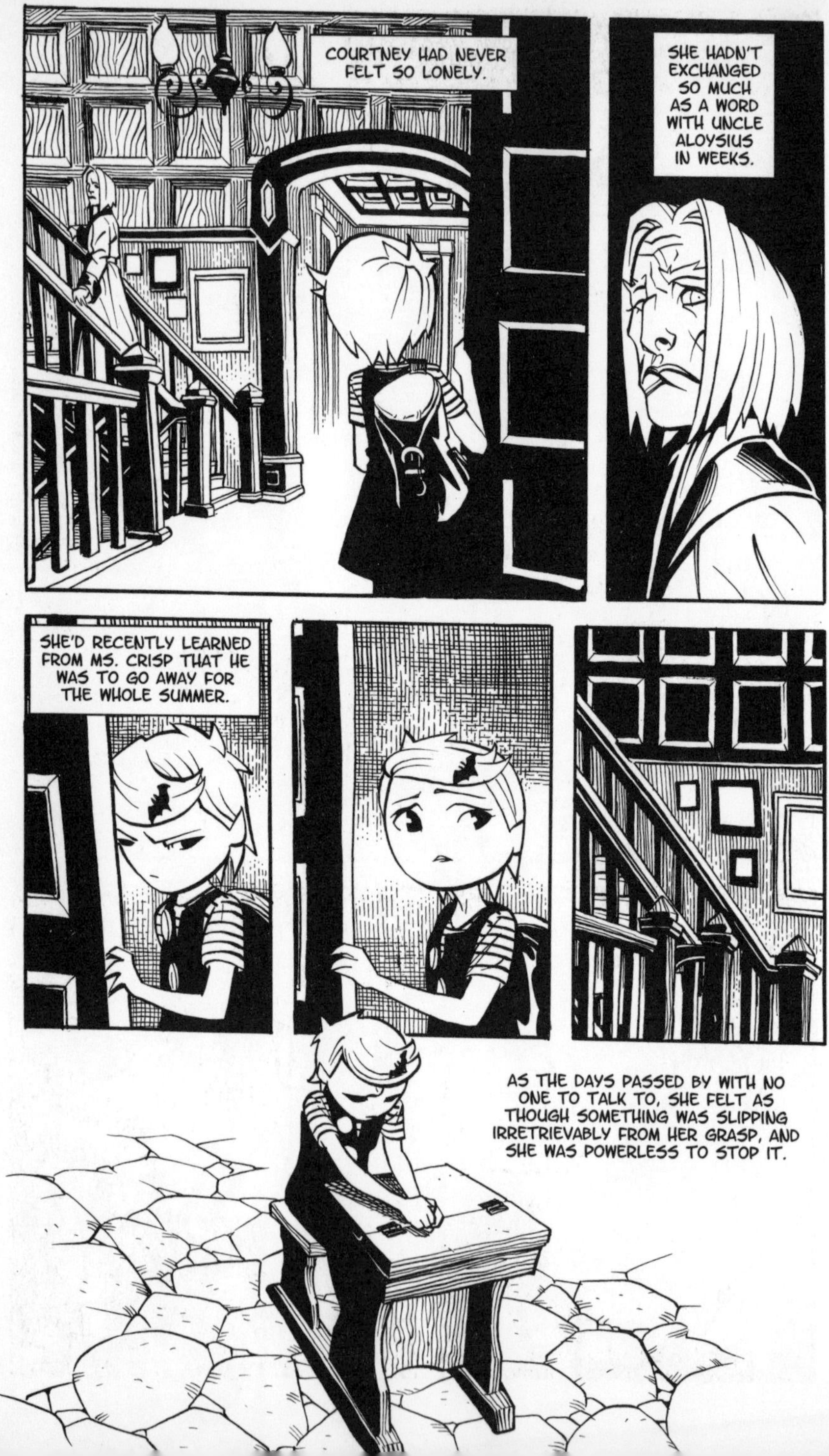

COURTNEY HAD NEVER FELT SO LONELY.
SHE HADN'T EXCHANGED SO MUCH AS A WORD WITH UNCLE ALOYSIUS IN WEEKS.
SHE'D RECENTLY LEARNED FROM MS. CRISP THAT HE WAS TO GO AWAY FOR THE WHOLE SUMMER.
AS THE DAYS PASSED BY WITH NO ONE TO TALK TO, SHE FELT AS THOUGH SOMETHING WAS SLIPPING IRRETRIEVABLY FROM HER GRASP, AND SHE WAS POWERLESS TO STOP IT.

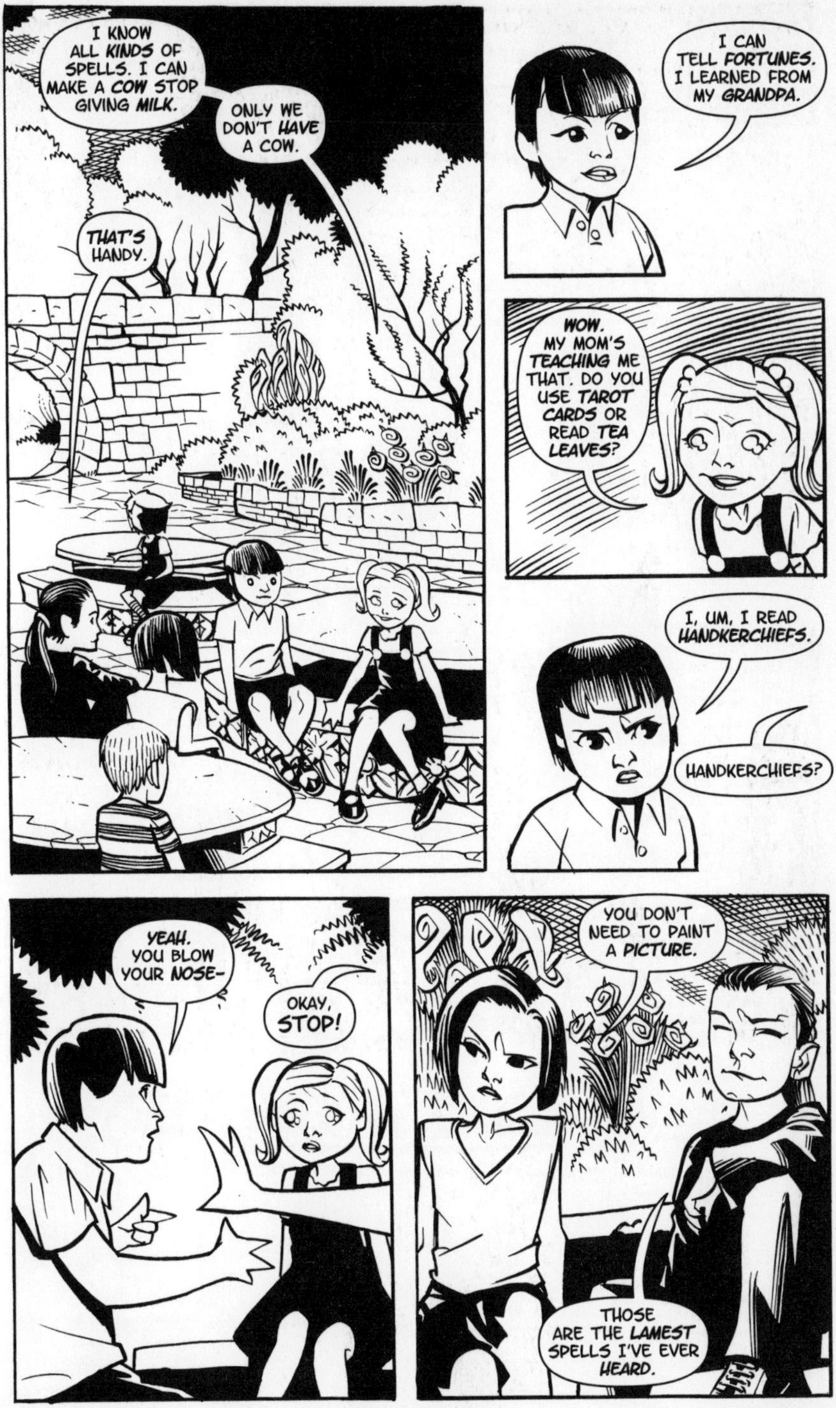

I KNOW ALL KINDS OF SPELLS. I CAN MAKE A COW STOP GIVING MILK.
ONLY WE DON'T HAVE A COW.
THAT'S HANDY.
I CAN TELL FORTUNES. I LEARNED FROM MY GRANDPA.
WOW. MY MOM'S TEACHING ME THAT. DO YOU USE TAROT CARDS OR READ TEA LEAVES?
I, UM, I READ HANDKERCHIEFS.
HANDKERCHIEFS?
YEAH. YOU BLOW YOUR NOSE-
OKAY, STOP!
YOU DON'T NEED TO PAINT A PICTURE.
THOSE ARE THE LAMEST SPELLS I'VE EVER HEARD.

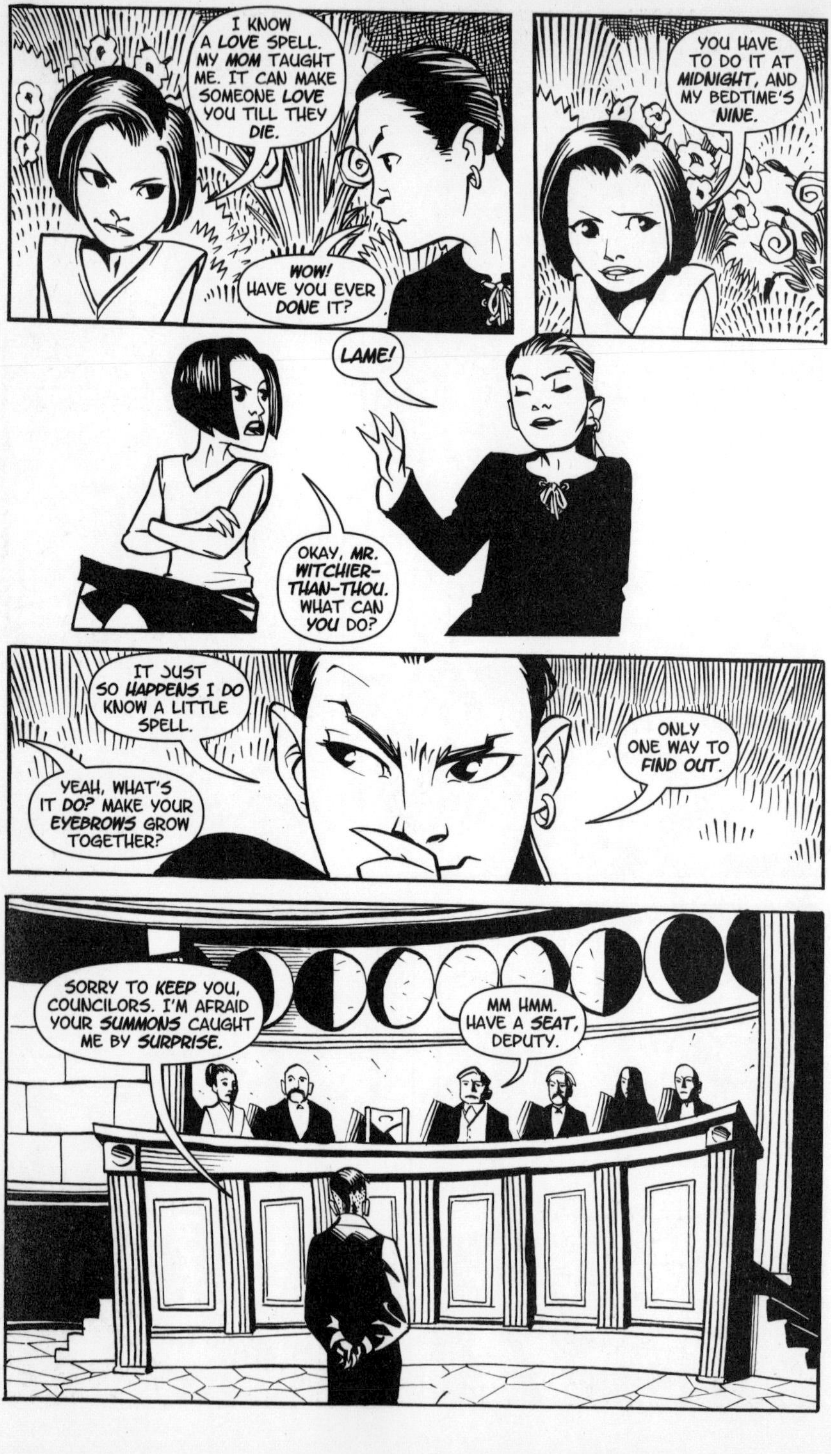
I KNOW A LOVE SPELL. MY MOM TAUGHT ME. IT CAN MAKE SOMEONE LOVE YOU TILL THEY DIE.
WOW! HAVE YOU EVER DONE IT?
YOU HAVE TO DO IT AT MIDNIGHT, AND MY BEDTIME'S NINE.
LAME!
OKAY, MR. WITCHIER-THAN-THOU. WHAT CAN YOU DO?
IT JUST SO HAPPENS I DO KNOW A LITTLE SPELL.
YEAH, WHAT'S IT DO? MAKE YOUR EYEBROWS GROW TOGETHER?
ONLY ONE WAY TO FIND OUT.
SORRY TO KEEP YOU, COUNCILORS. I'M AFRAID YOUR SUMMONS CAUGHT ME BY SURPRISE.
MM HMM. HAVE A SEAT, DEPUTY.

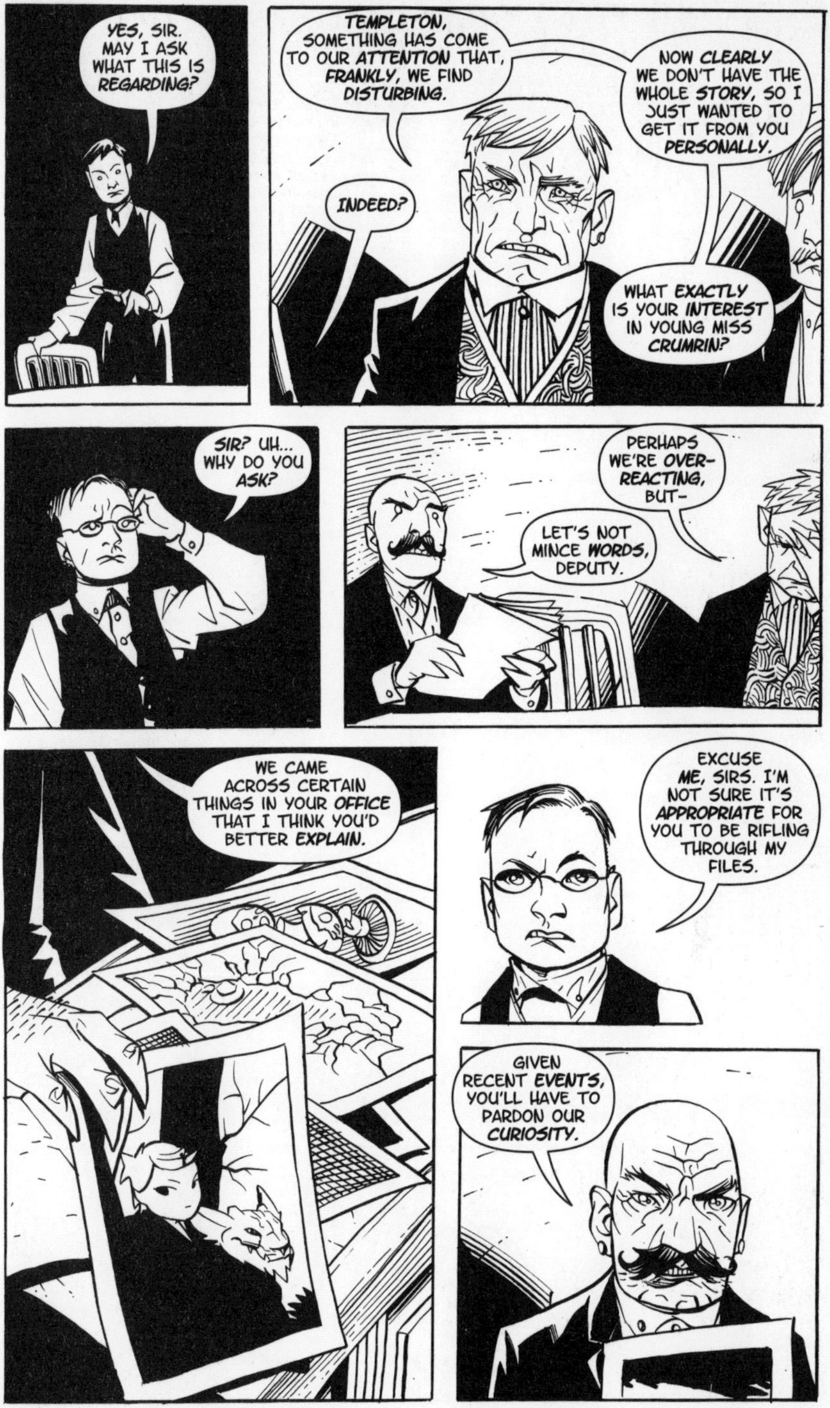
YES, SIR. MAY I ASK WHAT THIS IS REGARDING?
TEMPLETON, SOMETHING HAS COME TO OUR ATTENTION THAT, FRANKLY, WE FIND DISTURBING.
NOW CLEARLY WE DON'T HAVE THE WHOLE STORY, SO I JUST WANTED TO GET IT FROM YOU PERSONALLY.
INDEED?
WHAT EXACTLY IS YOUR INTEREST IN YOUNG MISS CRUMRIN?
SIR? UH... WHY DO YOU ASK?
PERHAPS WE'RE OVER-REACTING, BUT-
LET'S NOT MINCE WORDS, DEPUTY.
WE CAME ACROSS CERTAIN THINGS IN YOUR OFFICE THAT I THINK YOU'D BETTER EXPLAIN.
EXCUSE ME, SIRS. I'M NOT SURE IT'S APPROPRIATE FOR YOU TO BE RIFLING THROUGH MY FILES.
GIVEN RECENT EVENTS, YOU'LL HAVE TO PARDON OUR CURIOSITY.

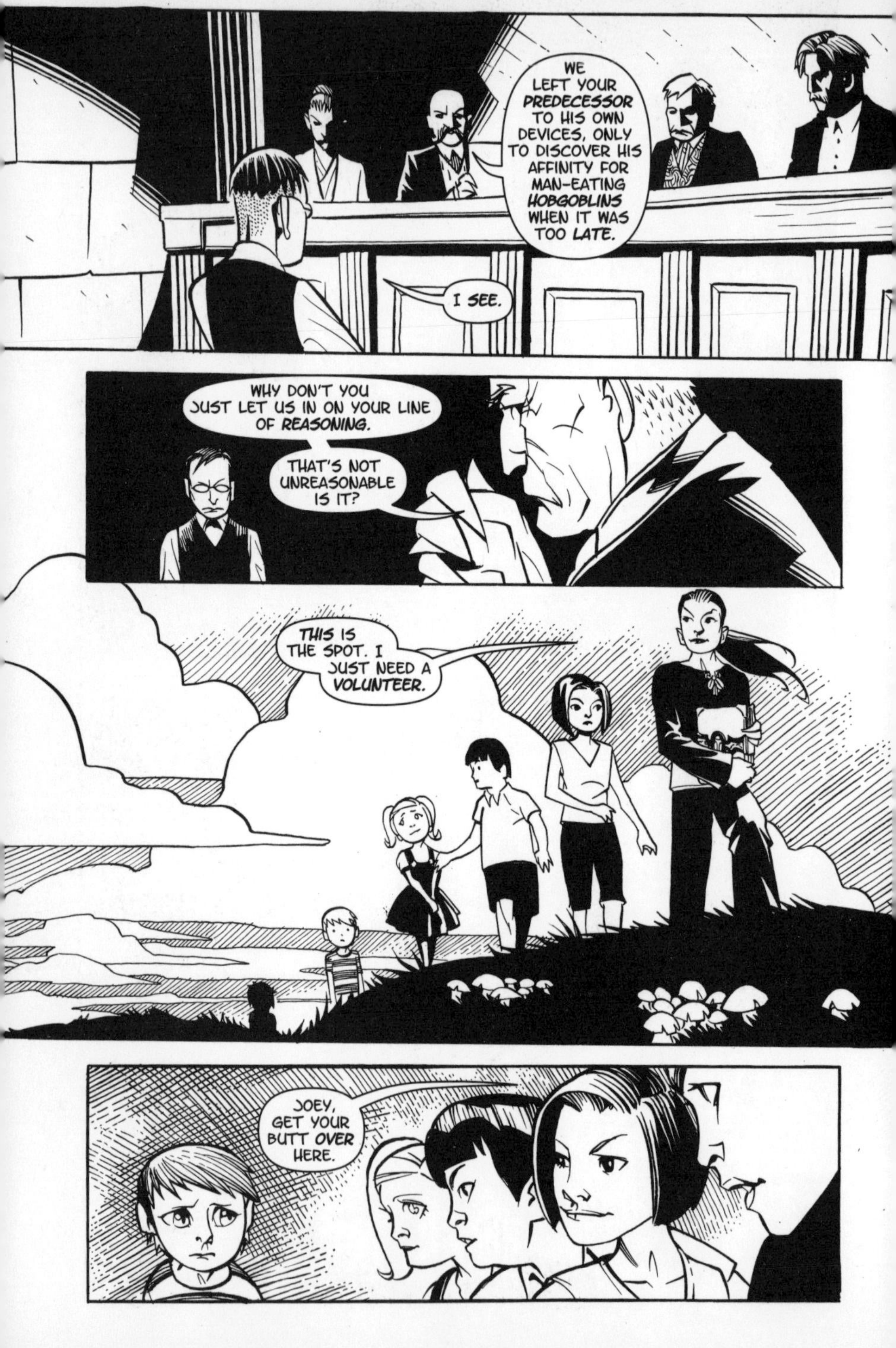
WE LEFT YOUR PREDECESSOR TO HIS OWN DEVICES, ONLY TO DISCOVER HIS AFFINITY FOR MAN-EATING HOBGOBLINS WHEN IT WAS TOO LATE.
I SEE.
WHY DON'T YOU JUST LET US IN ON YOUR LINE OF REASONING.
THAT'S NOT UNREASONABLE IS IT?
THIS IS THE SPOT. I JUST NEED A VOLUNTEER.
JOEY, GET YOUR BUTT OVER HERE.

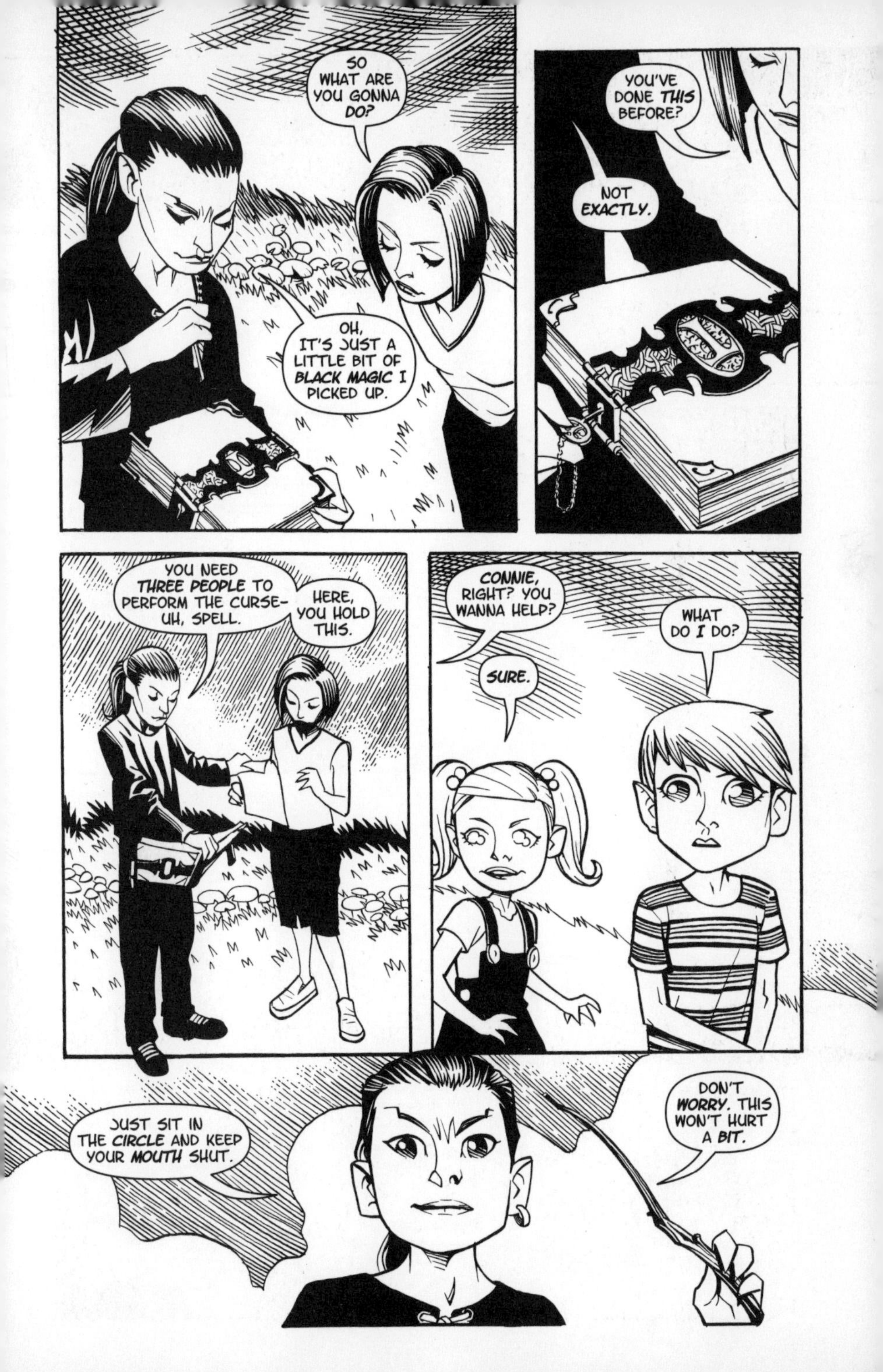
SO WHAT ARE YOU GONNA DO?
OH, IT'S JUST A LITTLE BIT OF BLACK MAGIC I PICKED UP.
YOU'VE DONE THIS BEFORE?
NOT EXACTLY.
YOU NEED THREE PEOPLE TO PERFORM THE CURSE-UH, SPELL.
HERE, YOU HOLD THIS.
CONNIE, RIGHT? YOU WANNA HELP?
SURE.
WHAT DO I DO?
JUST SIT IN THE CIRCLE AND KEEP YOUR MOUTH SHUT.
DON'T WORRY. THIS WON'T HURT A BIT.

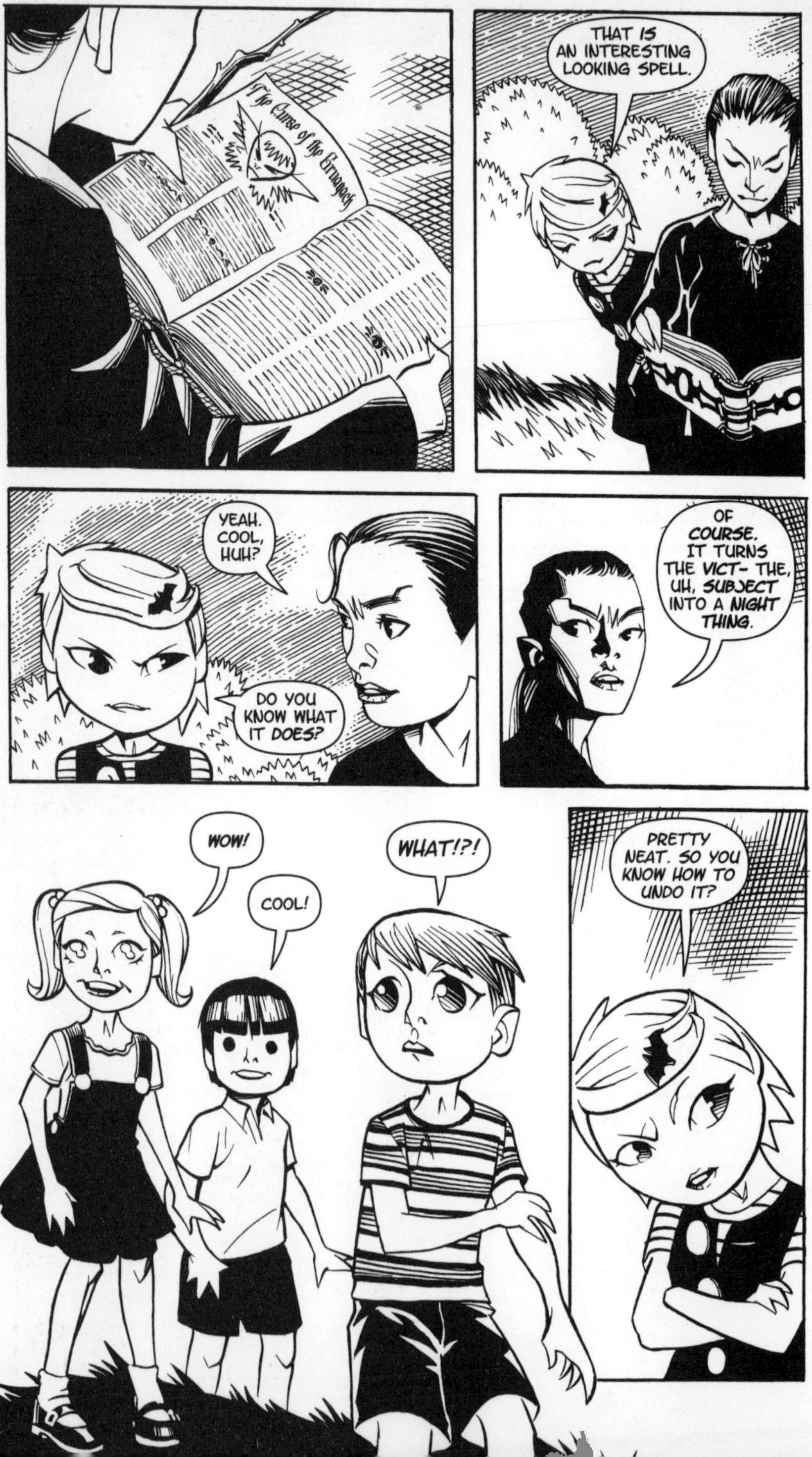
THAT IS AN INTERESTING LOOKING SPELL.
YEAH. COOL, HUH?
DO YOU KNOW WHAT IT DOES?
OF COURSE. IT TURNS THE VICT- THE, UH, SUBJECT INTO A NIGHT THING.
WOW!
COOL!
WHAT!?!
PRETTY NEAT. SO YOU KNOW HOW TO UNDO IT?

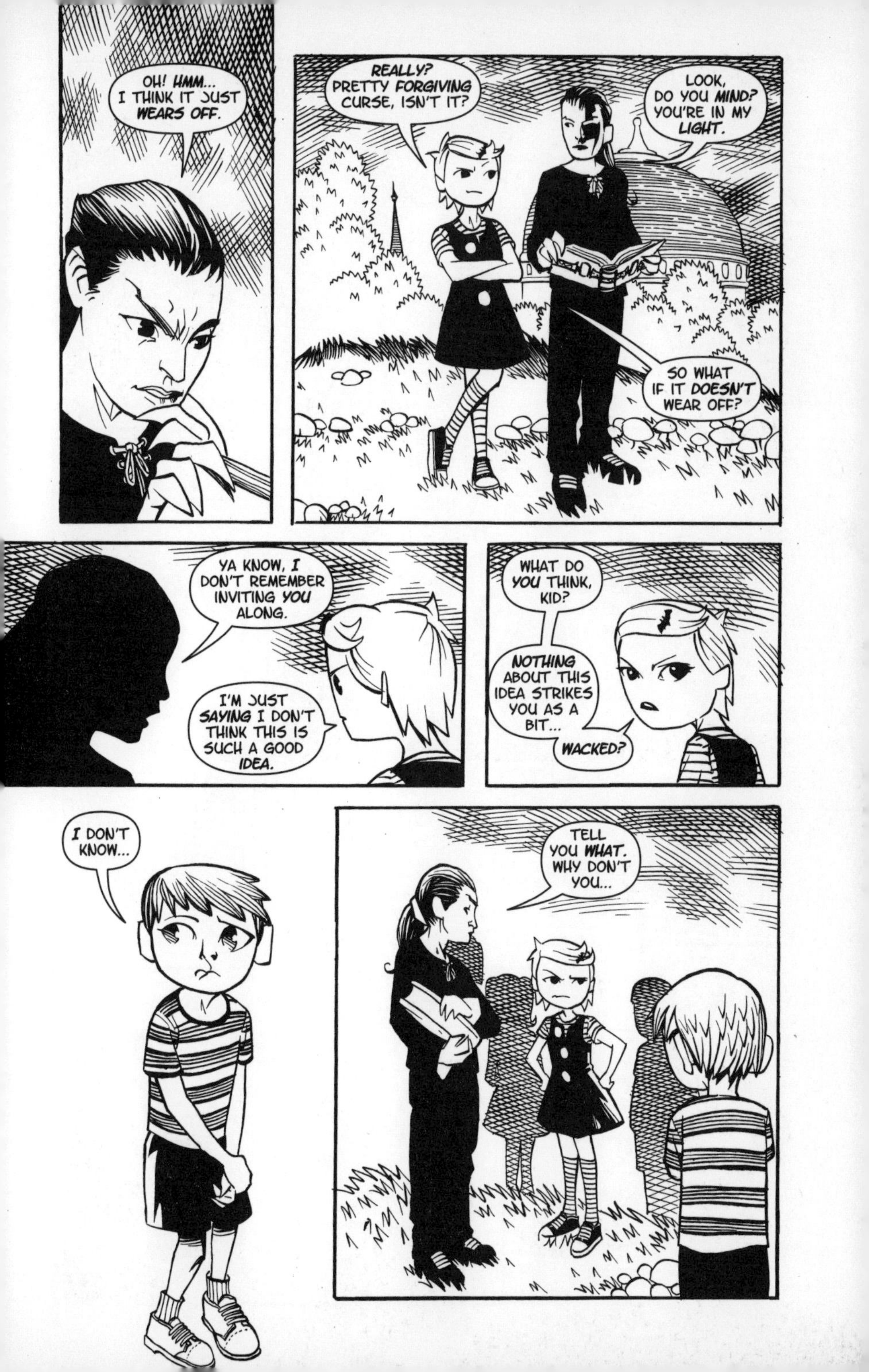
OH! HMM... I THINK IT JUST WEARS OFF.
REALLY? PRETTY FORGIVING CURSE, ISN'T IT?
LOOK, DO YOU MIND? YOU'RE IN MY LIGHT.
SO WHAT IF IT DOESN'T WEAR OFF?
YA KNOW, I DON'T REMEMBER INVITING YOU ALONG.
I'M JUST SAYING I DON'T THINK THIS IS SUCH A GOOD IDEA.
WHAT DO YOU THINK, KID?
NOTHING ABOUT THIS IDEA STRIKES YOU AS A BIT...
WACKED?
I DON'T KNOW...
TELL YOU WHAT. WHY DON'T YOU...

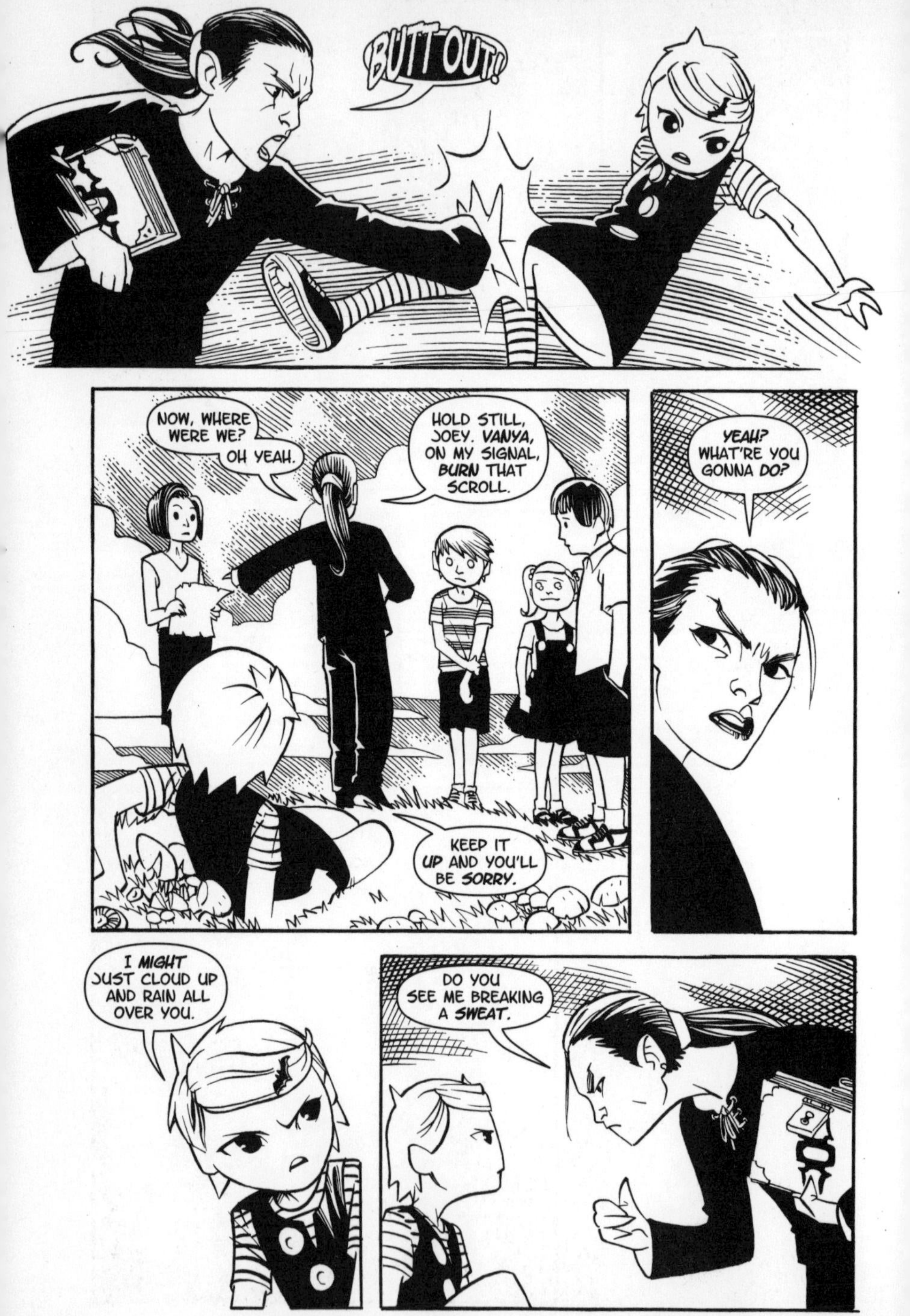
BUTT OUT!!
NOW, WHERE WERE WE? OH YEAH.
HOLD STILL, JOEY. VANYA, ON MY SIGNAL, BURN THAT SCROLL.
KEEP IT UP AND YOU'LL BE SORRY.
YEAH? WHAT'RE YOU GONNA DO?
I MIGHT JUST CLOUD UP AND RAIN ALL OVER YOU.
DO YOU SEE ME BREAKING A SWEAT.

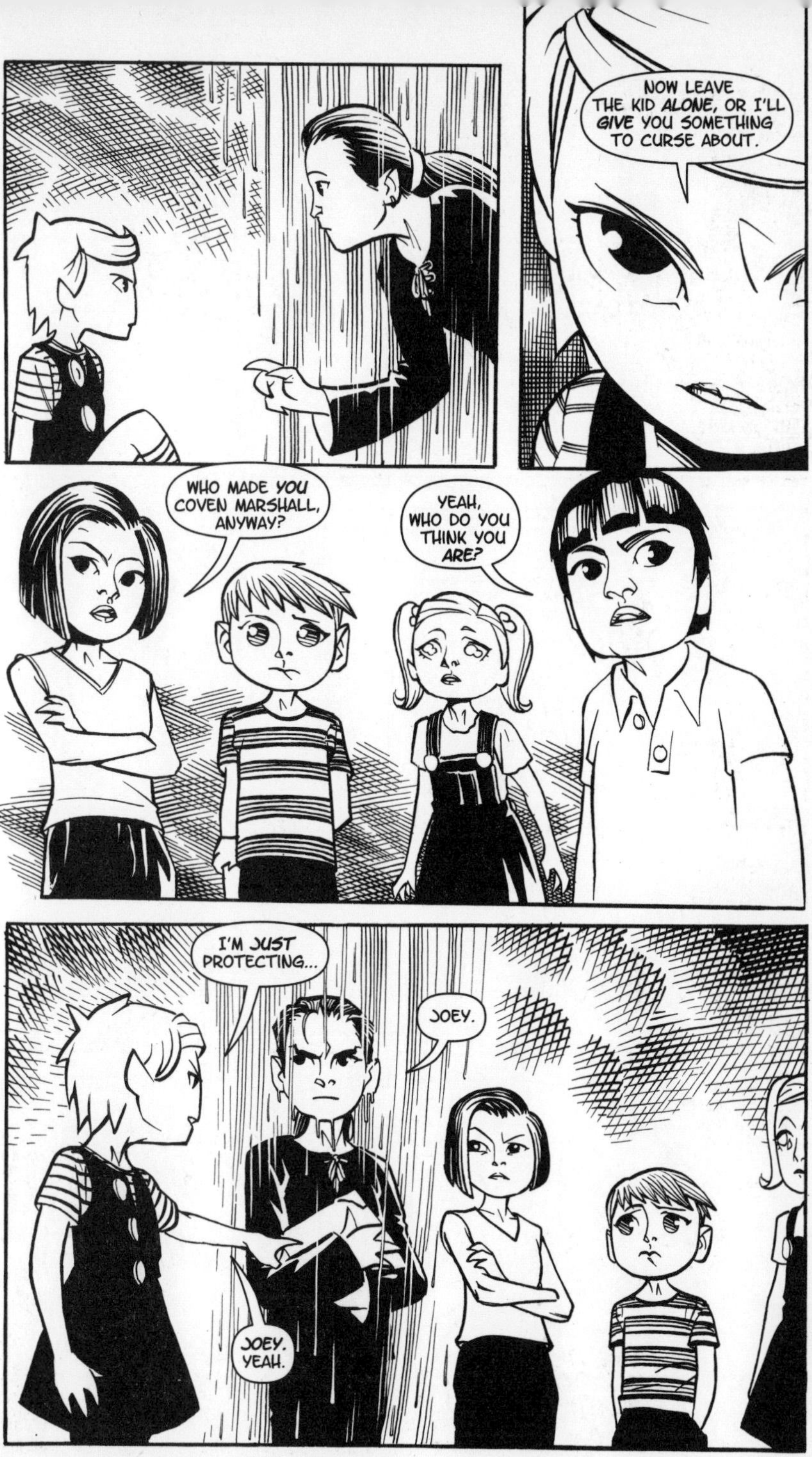
NOW LEAVE THE KID ALONE, OR I'LL GIVE YOU SOMETHING TO CURSE ABOUT.
WHO MADE YOU COVEN MARSHALL, ANYWAY?
YEAH, WHO DO YOU THINK YOU ARE?
I'M JUST PROTECTING...
JOEY.
JOEY. YEAH.

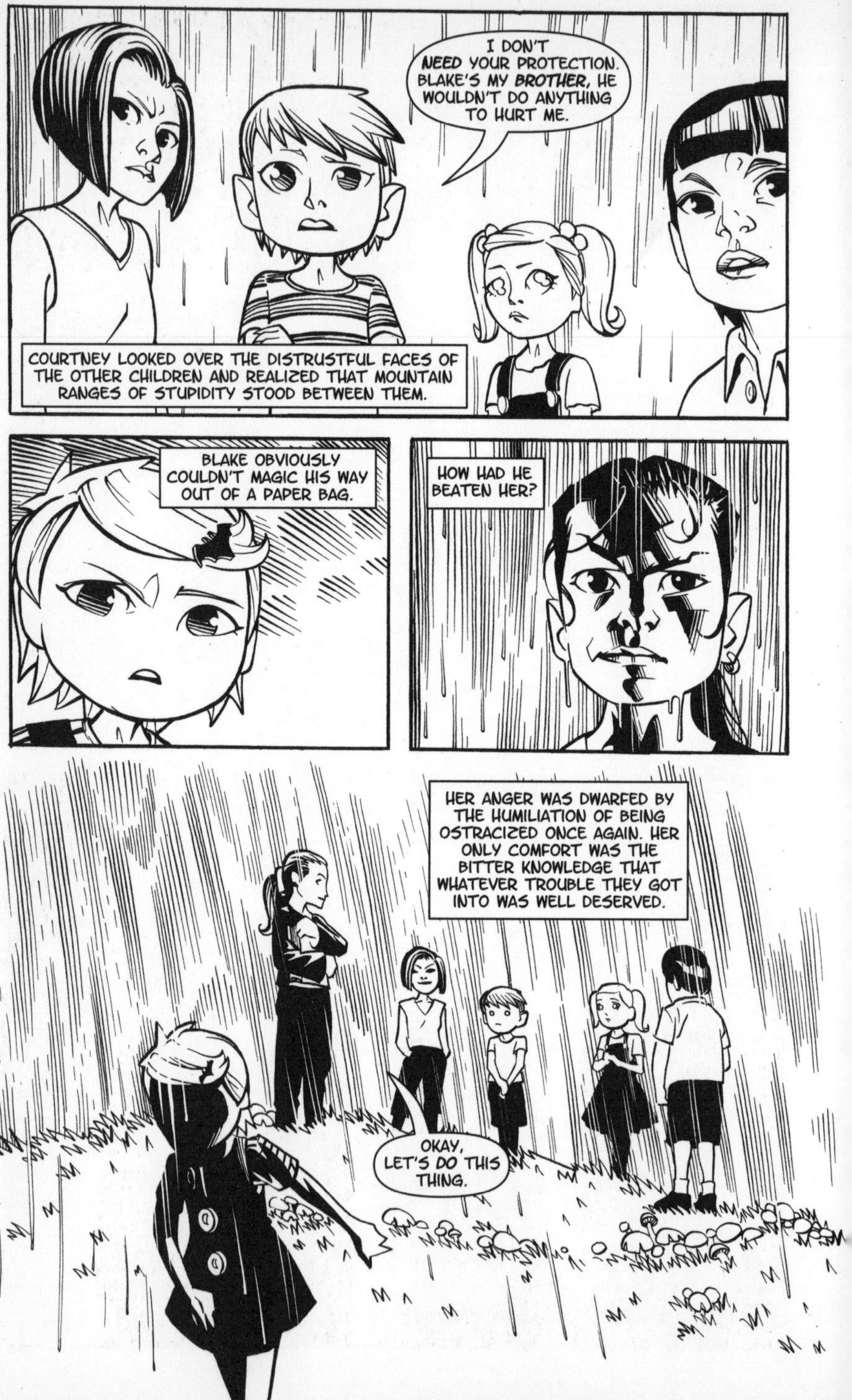
I DON'T NEED YOUR PROTECTION. BLAKE'S MY BROTHER, HE WOULDN'T DO ANYTHING TO HURT ME.
COURTNEY LOOKED OVER THE DISTRUSTFUL FACES OF THE OTHER CHILDREN AND REALIZED THAT MOUNTAIN RANGES OF STUPIDITY STOOD BETWEEN THEM.
BLAKE OBVIOUSLY COULDN'T MAGIC HIS WAY OUT OF A PAPER BAG.
HOW HAD HE BEATEN HER?
HER ANGER WAS DWARFED BY THE HUMILIATION OF BEING OSTRACIZED ONCE AGAIN. HER ONLY COMFORT WAS THE BITTER KNOWLEDGE THAT WHATEVER TROUBLE THEY GOT INTO WAS WELL DESERVED.
OKAY, LET'S DO THIS THING.

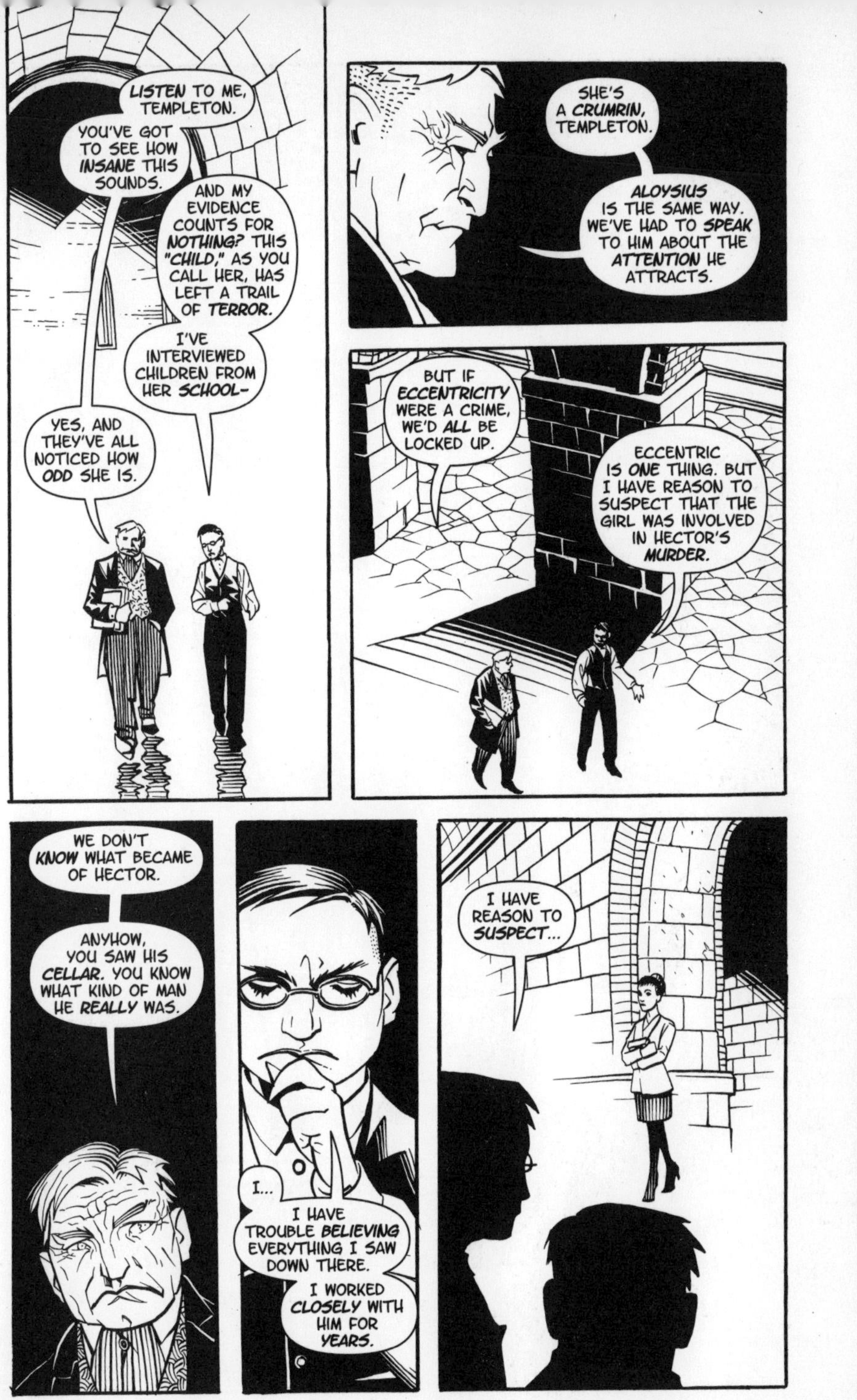
LISTEN TO ME, TEMPLETON.
YOU'VE GOT TO SEE HOW INSANE THIS SOUNDS.
AND MY EVIDENCE COUNTS FOR NOTHING? THIS "CHILD," AS YOU CALL HER, HAS LEFT A TRAIL OF TERROR.
I'VE INTERVIEWED CHILDREN FROM HER SCHOOL-
YES, AND THEY'VE ALL NOTICED HOW ODD SHE IS.
SHE'S A CRUMRIN, TEMPLETON.
ALOYSIUS IS THE SAME WAY. WE'VE HAD TO SPEAK TO HIM ABOUT THE ATTENTION HE ATTRACTS.
BUT IF ECCENTRICITY WERE A CRIME, WE'D ALL BE LOCKED UP.
ECCENTRIC IS ONE THING. BUT I HAVE REASON TO SUSPECT THAT THE GIRL WAS INVOLVED IN HECTOR'S MURDER.
WE DON'T KNOW WHAT BECAME OF HECTOR.
ANYHOW, YOU SAW HIS CELLAR. YOU KNOW WHAT KIND OF MAN HE REALLY WAS.
I...
I HAVE TROUBLE BELIEVING EVERYTHING I SAW DOWN THERE.
I WORKED CLOSELY WITH HIM FOR YEARS.
I HAVE REASON TO SUSPECT...

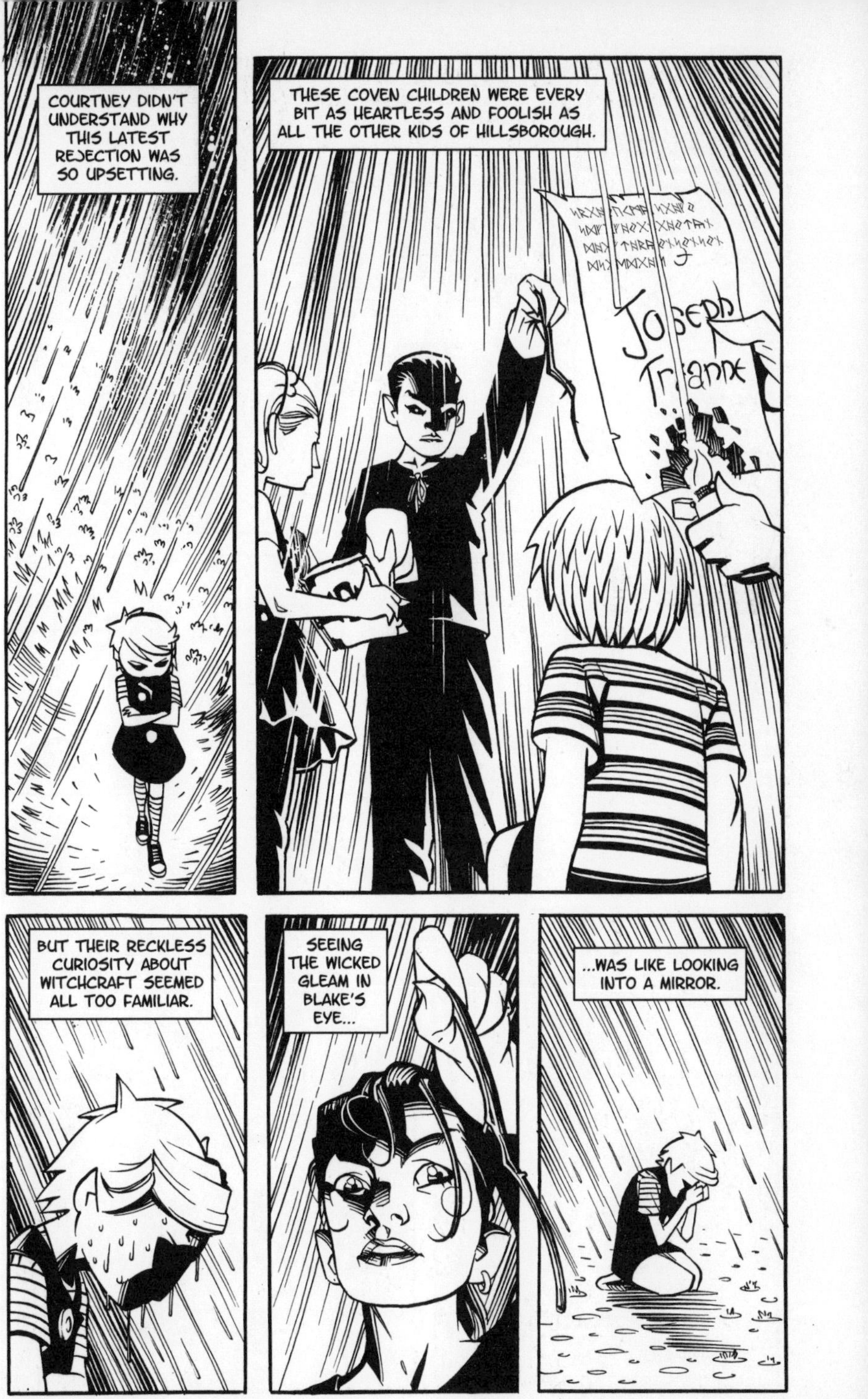
COURTNEY DIDN'T UNDERSTAND WHY THIS LATEST REJECTION WAS SO UPSETTING.
THESE COVEN CHILDREN WERE EVERY BIT AS HEARTLESS AND FOOLISH AS ALL THE OTHER KIDS OF HILLSBOROUGH.
BUT THEIR RECKLESS CURIOSITY ABOUT WITCHCRAFT SEEMED ALL TOO FAMILIAR.
SEEING THE WICKED GLEAM IN BLAKE'S EYE...
...WAS LIKE LOOKING INTO A MIRROR.

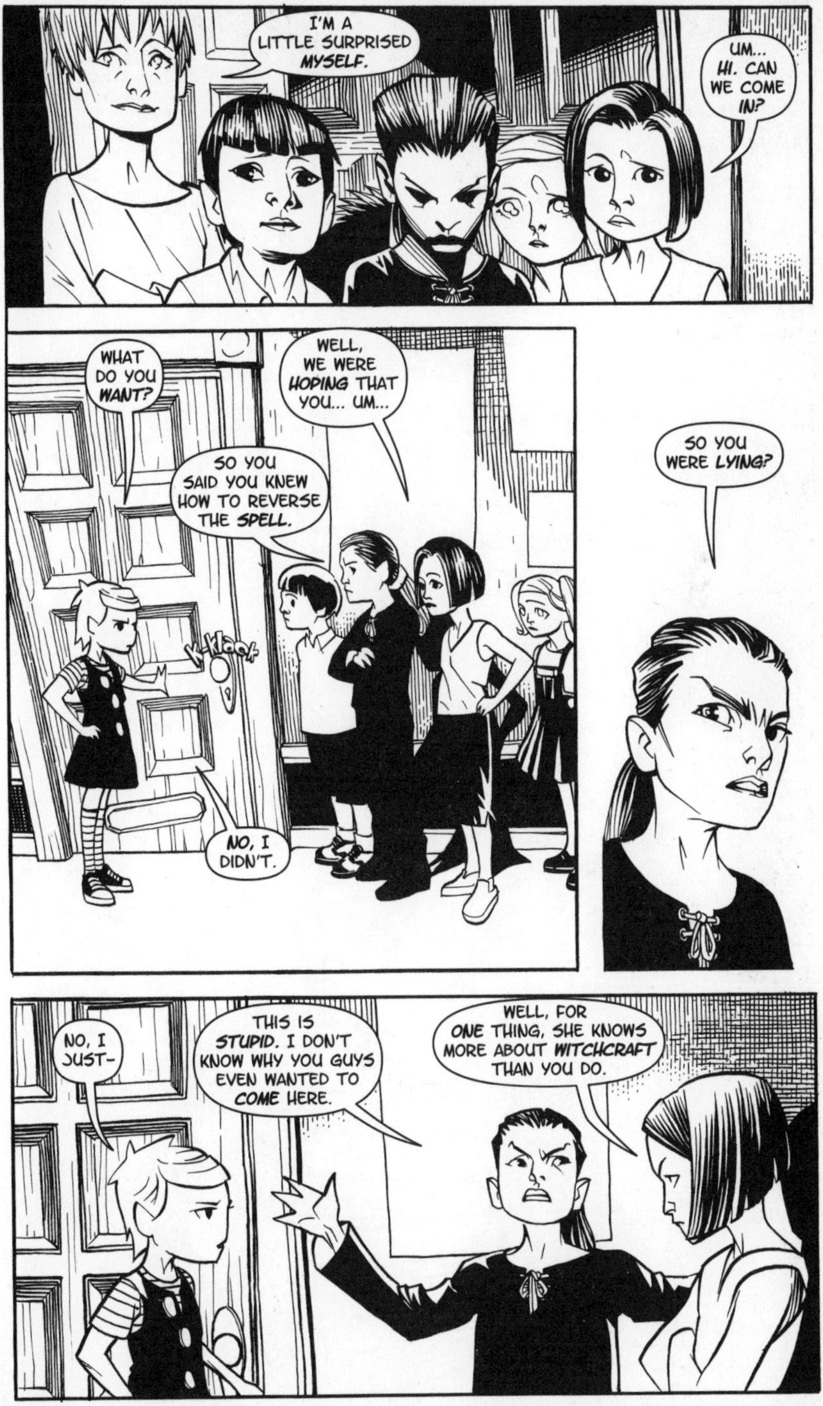
I'M A LITTLE SURPRISED MYSELF.
UM... HI. CAN WE COME IN?
WHAT DO YOU WANT?
WELL, WE WERE HOPING THAT YOU... UM...
SO YOU SAID YOU KNEW HOW TO REVERSE THE SPELL.
NO, I DIDN'T.
SO YOU WERE LYING?
NO, I JUST-
THIS IS STUPID. I DON'T KNOW WHY YOU GUYS EVEN WANTED TO COME HERE.
WELL, FOR ONE THING, SHE KNOWS MORE ABOUT WITCHCRAFT THAN YOU DO.

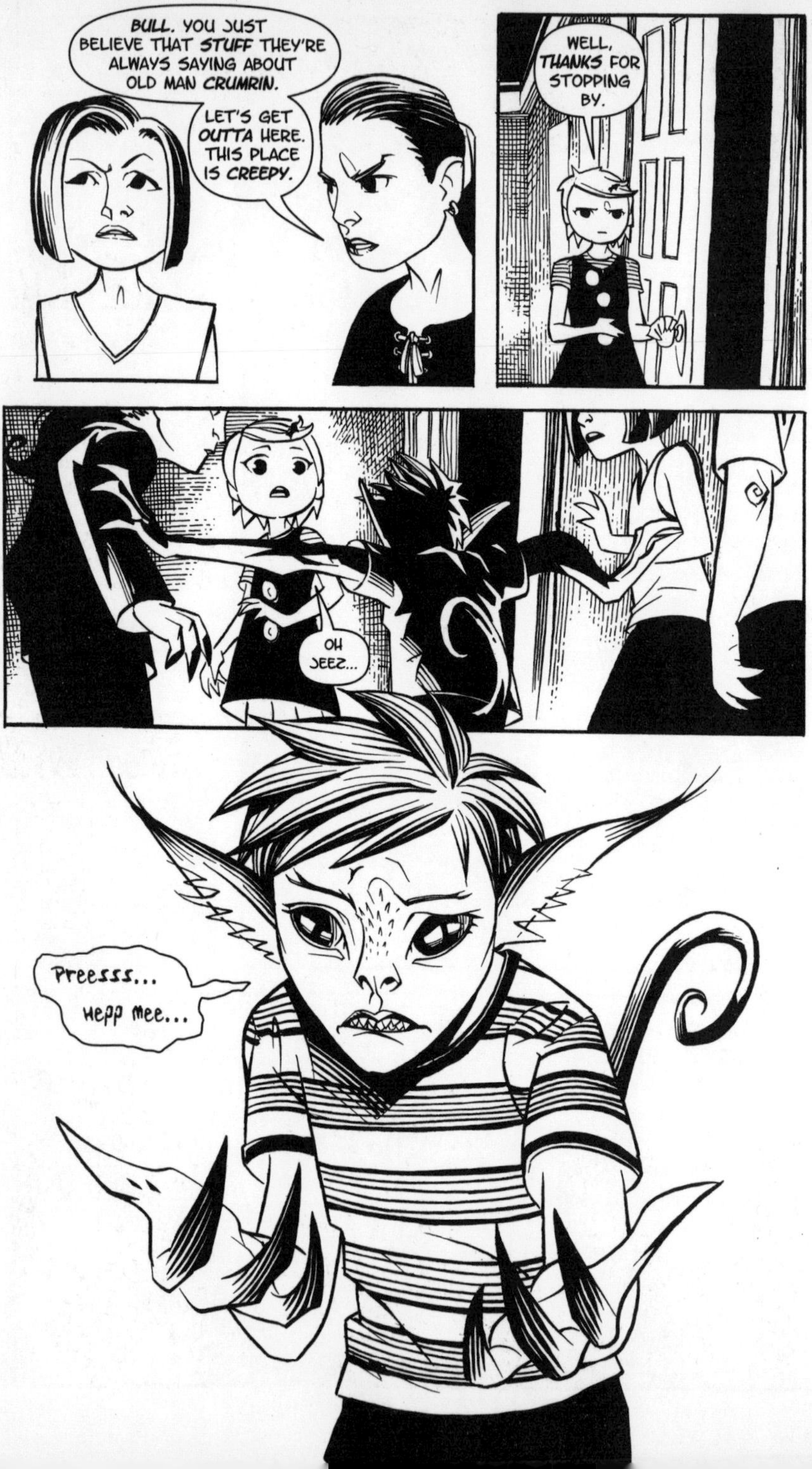

BULL. YOU JUST BELIEVE THAT STUFF THEY'RE ALWAYS SAYING ABOUT OLD MAN CRUMRIN.
LET'S GET OUTTA HERE. THIS PLACE IS CREEPY.
WELL, THANKS FOR STOPPING BY.
OH JEEZ...
Preessss...
Hepp mee...

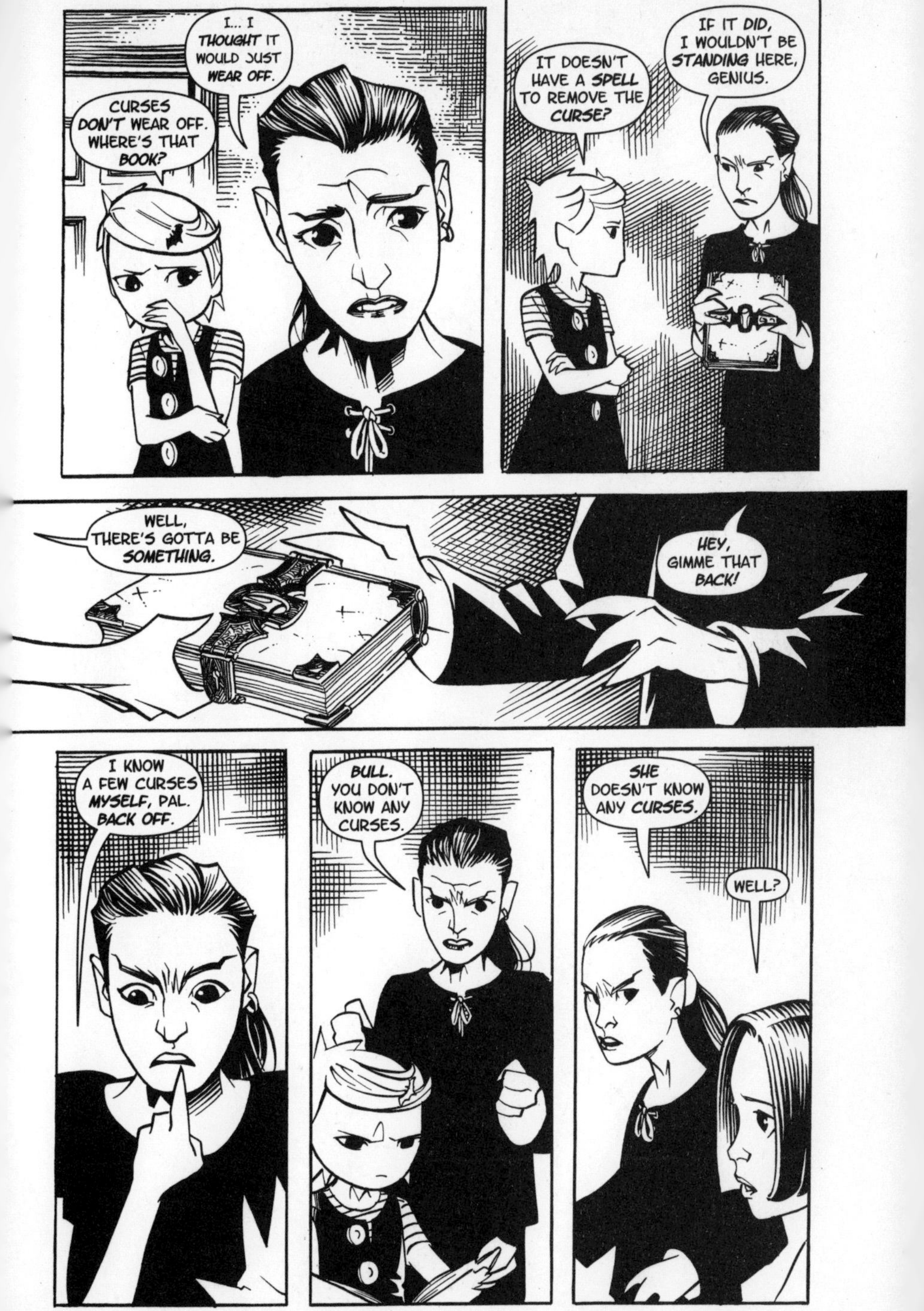
I... I THOUGHT IT WOULD JUST WEAR OFF.
CURSES DON'T WEAR OFF. WHERE'S THAT BOOK?
IT DOESN'T HAVE A SPELL TO REMOVE THE CURSE?
IF IT DID, I WOULDN'T BE STANDING HERE, GENIUS.
WELL, THERE'S GOTTA BE SOMETHING.
HEY, GIMME THAT BACK!
I KNOW A FEW CURSES MYSELF, PAL. BACK OFF.
BULL. YOU DON'T KNOW ANY CURSES.
SHE DOESN'T KNOW ANY CURSES.
WELL?

CHAPTER THREE

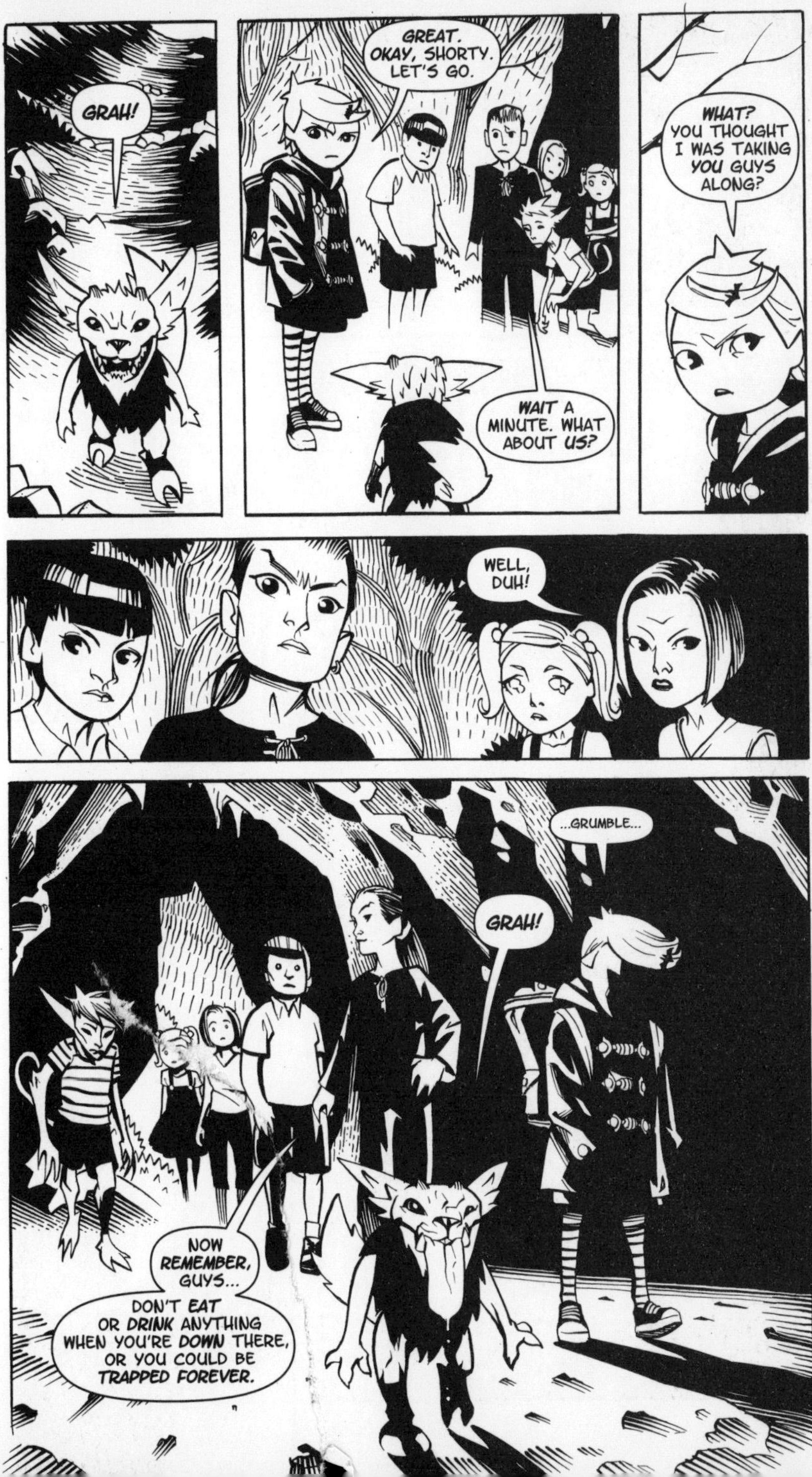
GRAH!
GREAT. OKAY, SHORTY. LET'S GO.
WAIT A MINUTE. WHAT ABOUT US?
WHAT? YOU THOUGHT I WAS TAKING YOU GUYS ALONG?
WELL, DUH!
...GRUMBLE...
GRAH!
NOW REMEMBER, GUYS...
DON'T EAT OR DRINK ANYTHING WHEN YOU'RE DOWN THERE, OR YOU COULD BE TRAPPED FOREVER.

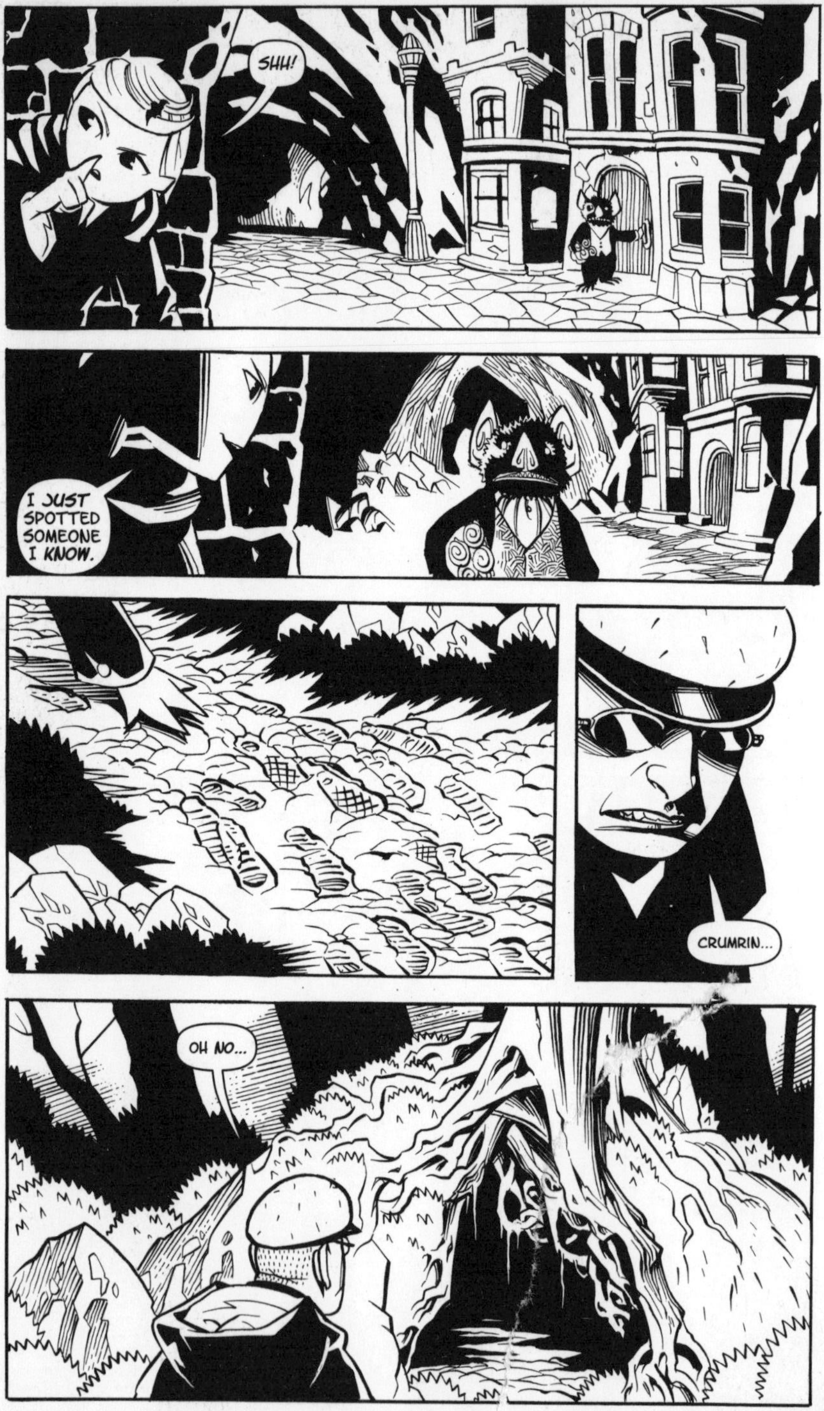
SHH!
I JUST SPOTTED SOMEONE I KNOW.
CRUMRIN...
OH NO...

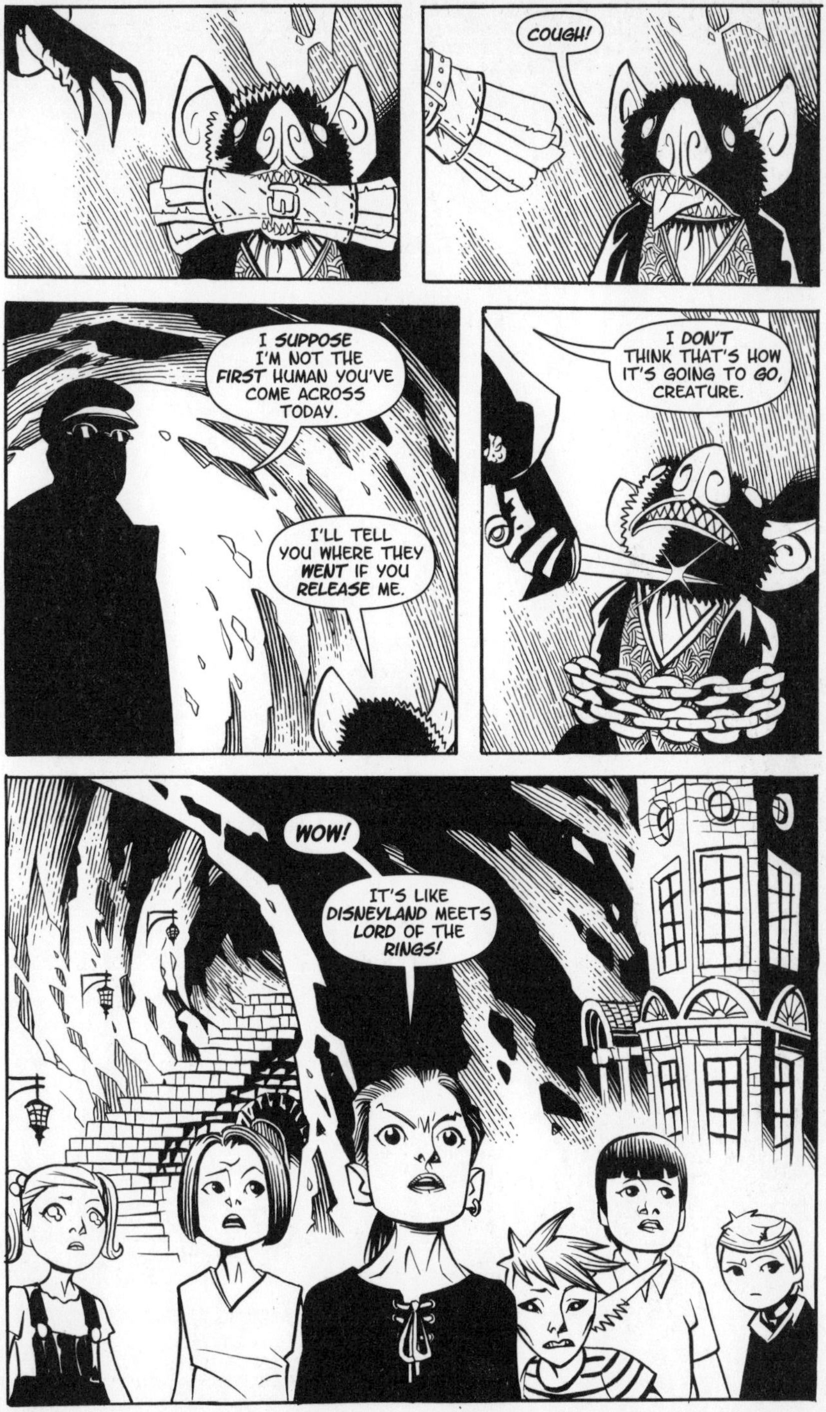
COUGH!
I SUPPOSE I'M NOT THE FIRST HUMAN YOU'VE COME ACROSS TODAY.
I'LL TELL YOU WHERE THEY WENT IF YOU RELEASE ME.
I DON'T THINK THAT'S HOW IT'S GOING TO GO, CREATURE.
WOW!
IT'S LIKE DISNEYLAND MEETS LORD OF THE RINGS!

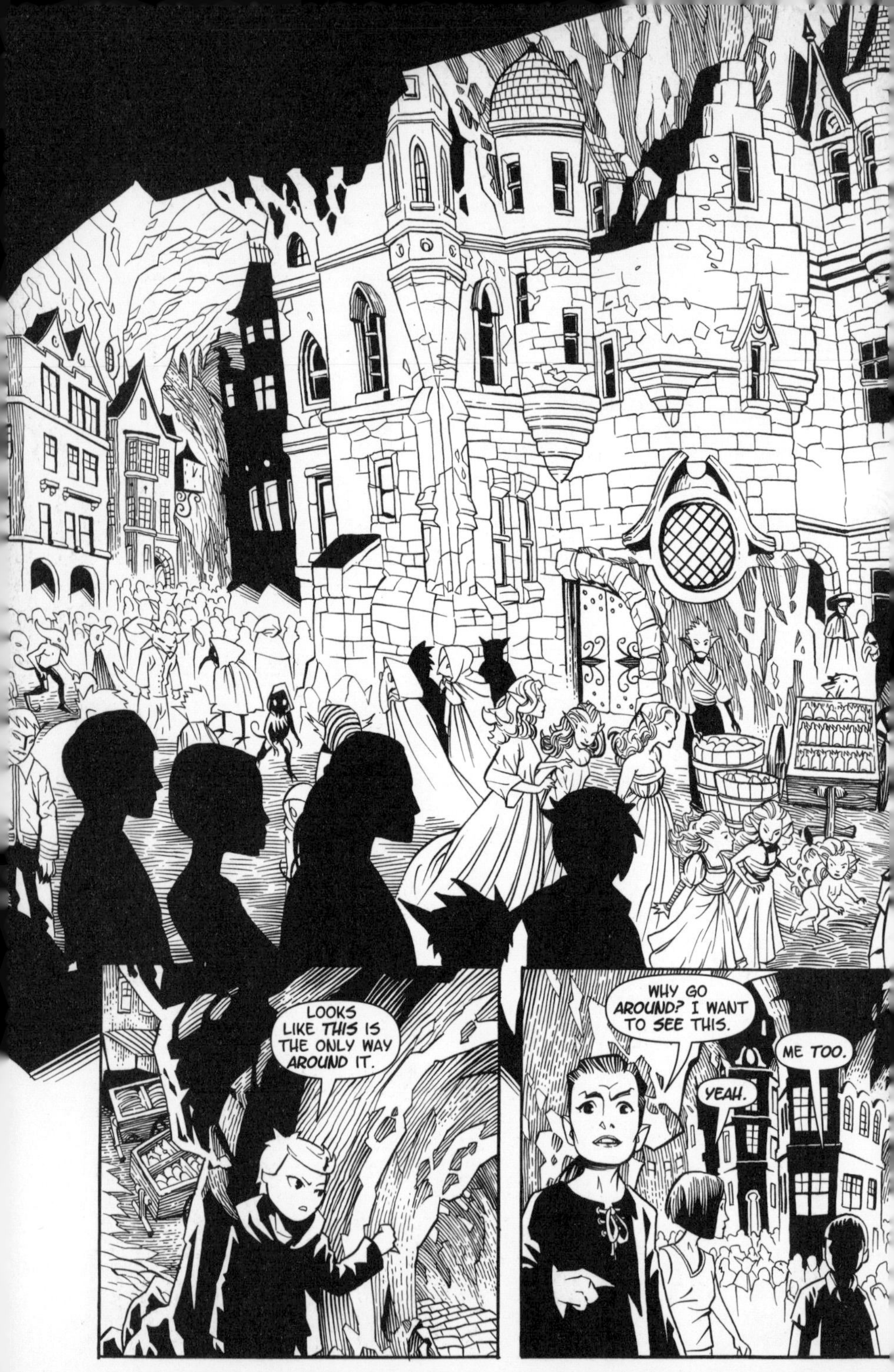
LOOKS LIKE THIS IS THE ONLY WAY AROUND IT.
WHY GO AROUND? I WANT TO SEE THIS.
YEAH.
ME TOO.

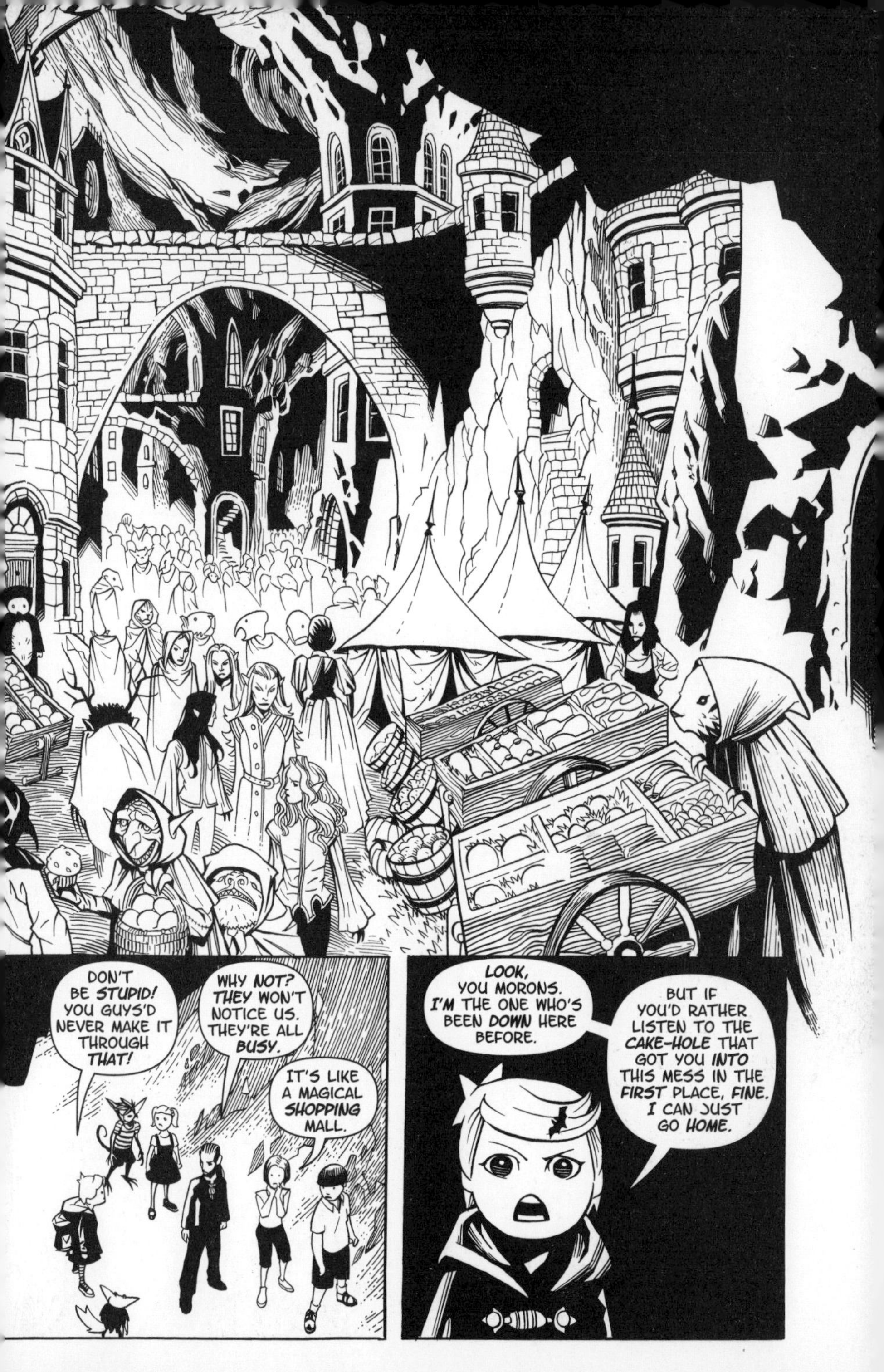
DON'T BE STUPID! YOU GUYS'D NEVER MAKE IT THROUGH THAT!
WHY NOT? THEY WON'T NOTICE US. THEY'RE ALL BUSY.
IT'S LIKE A MAGICAL SHOPPING MALL.
LOOK, YOU MORONS. I'M THE ONE WHO'S BEEN DOWN HERE BEFORE.
BUT IF YOU'D RATHER LISTEN TO THE CAKE-HOLE THAT GOT YOU INTO THIS MESS IN THE FIRST PLACE, FINE. I CAN JUST GO HOME.

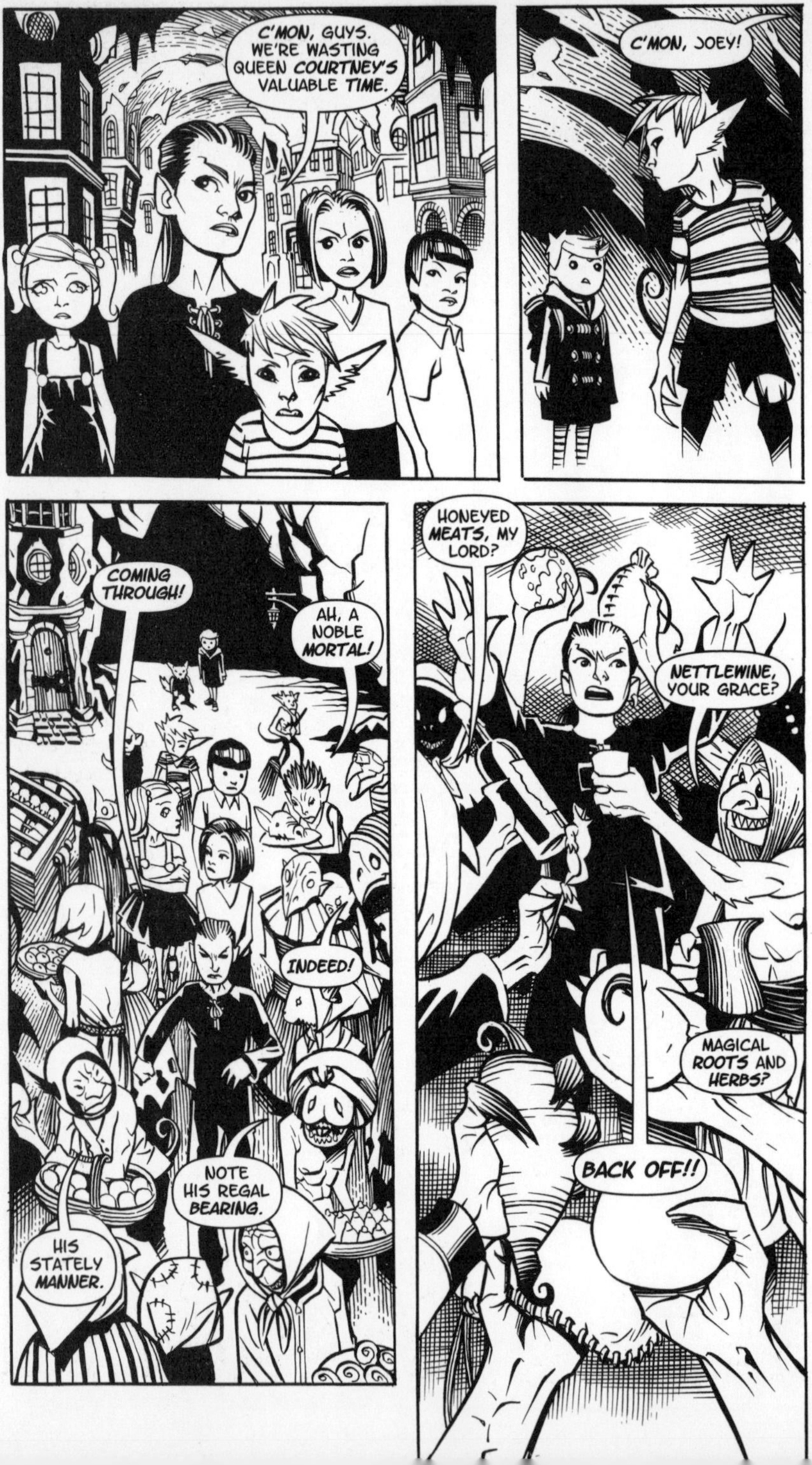
C'MON, GUYS. WE'RE WASTING QUEEN COURTNEY'S VALUABLE TIME.
C'MON, JOEY!
COMING THROUGH!
AH, A NOBLE MORTAL!
INDEED!
NOTE HIS REGAL BEARING.
HIS STATELY MANNER.
HONEYED MEATS, MY LORD?
NETTLEWINE, YOUR GRACE?
MAGICAL ROOTS AND HERBS?
BACK OFF!!

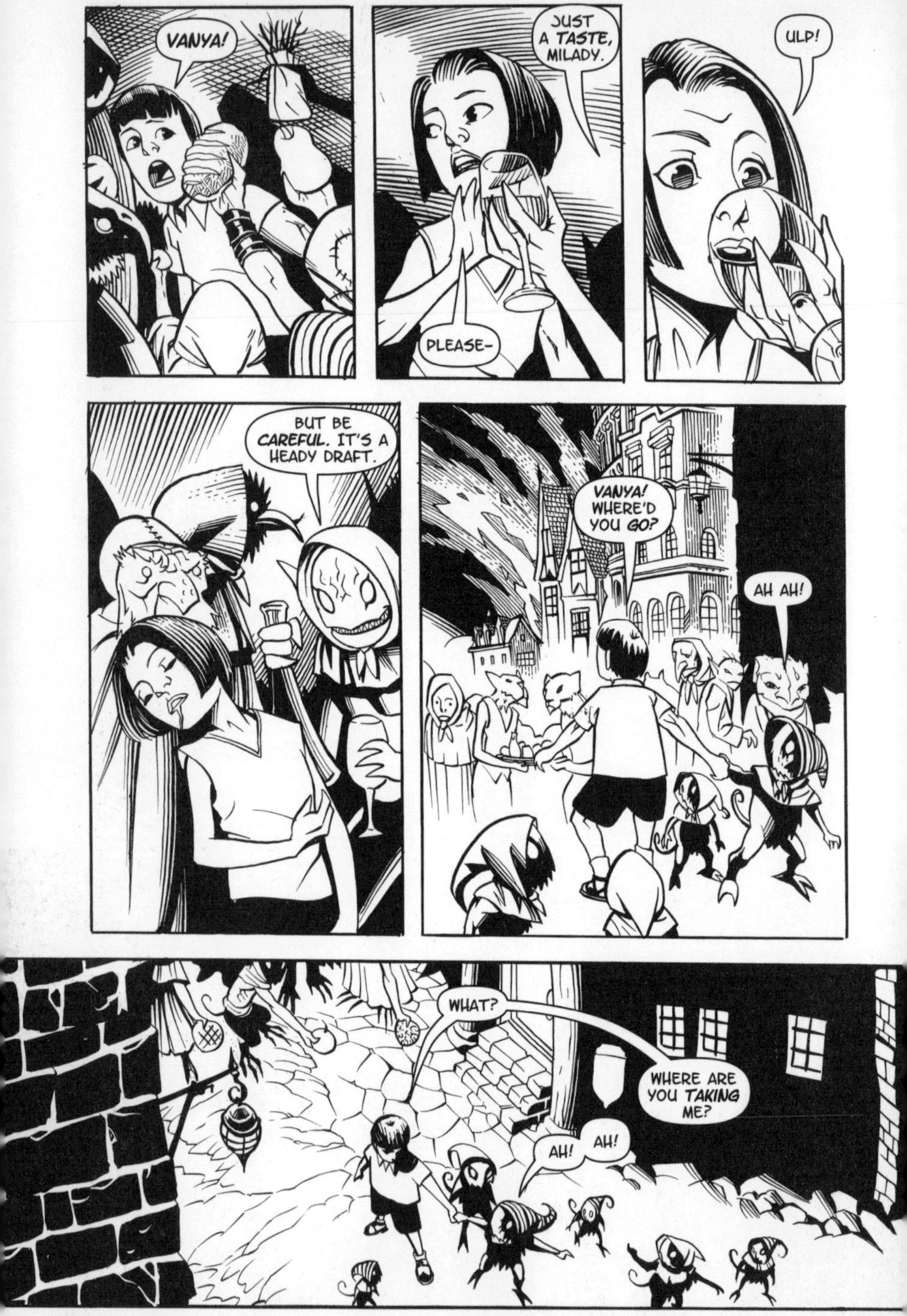
VANYA!
JUST A TASTE, MILADY.
PLEASE-
ULP!
BUT BE CAREFUL. IT'S A HEADY DRAFT.
VANYA! WHERE'D YOU GO?
AH AH!
WHAT?
WHERE ARE YOU TAKING ME?
AH!
AH!

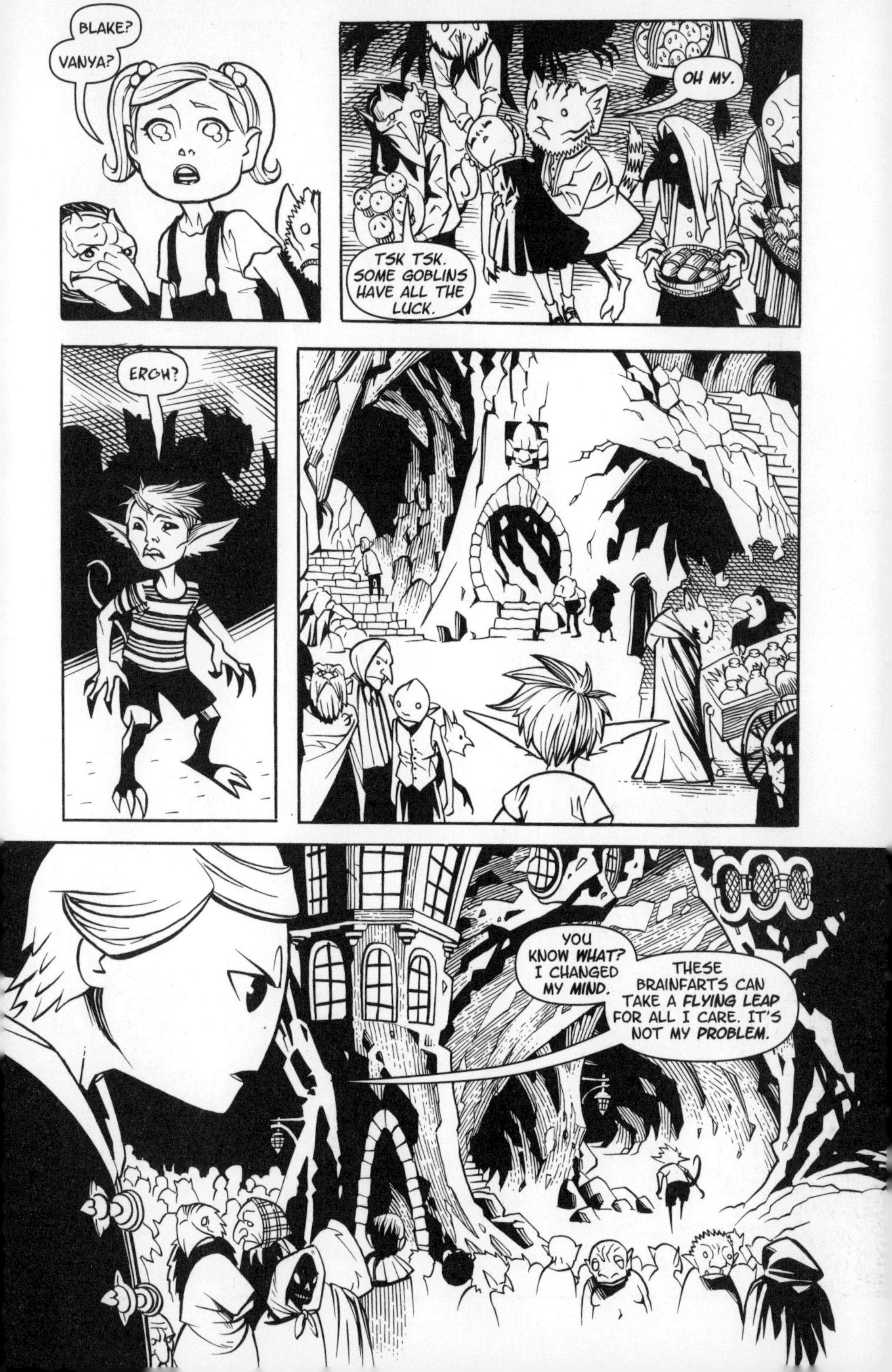
BLAKE?
VANYA?
OH MY.
TSK TSK. SOME GOBLINS HAVE ALL THE LUCK.
ERGH?
YOU KNOW WHAT? I CHANGED MY MIND.
THESE BRAINFARTS CAN TAKE A FLYING LEAP FOR ALL I CARE. IT'S NOT MY PROBLEM.

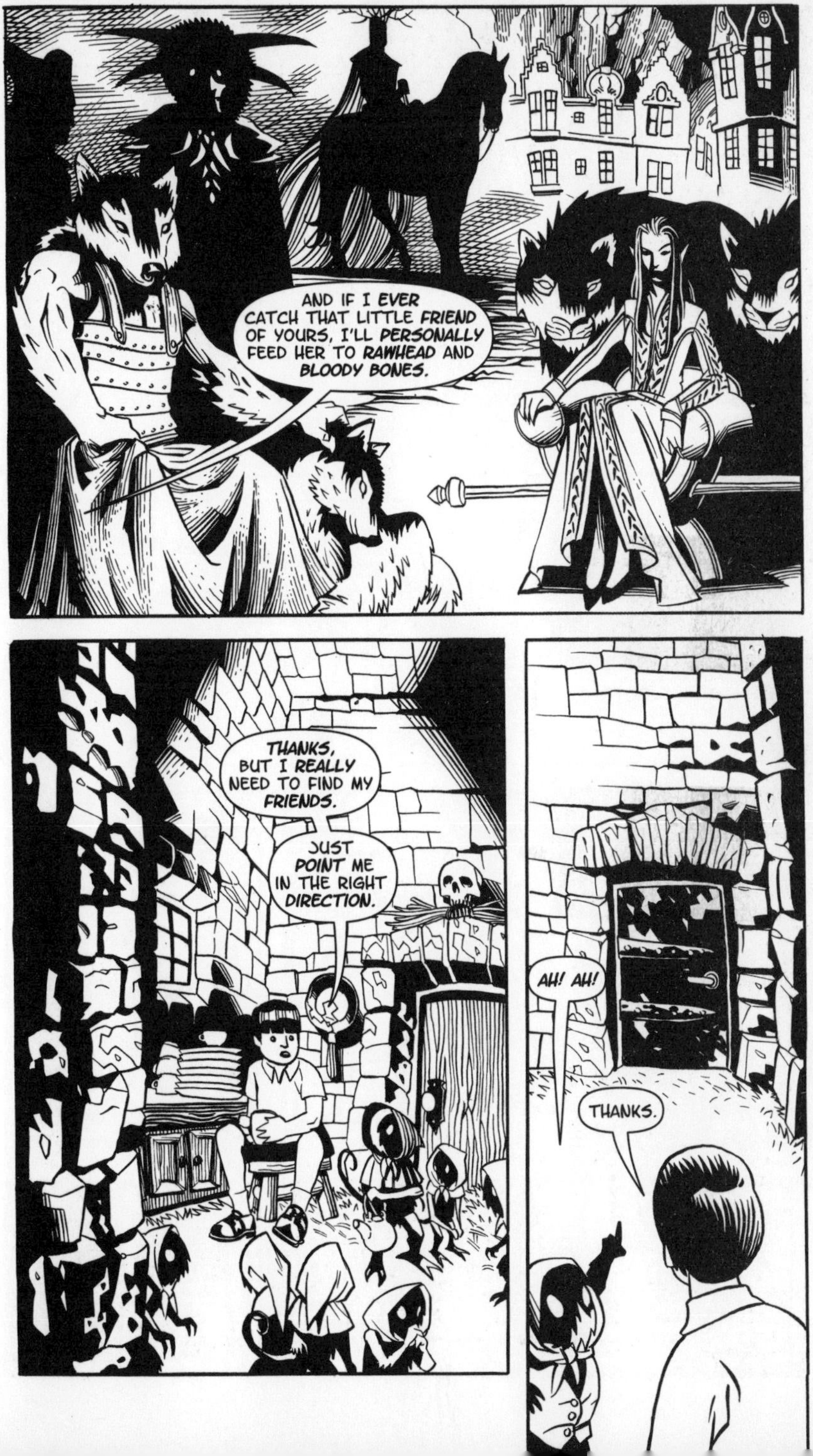
AND IF I EVER CATCH THAT LITTLE FRIEND OF YOURS, I'LL PERSONALLY FEED HER TO RAWHEAD AND BLOODY BONES.
THANKS, BUT I REALLY NEED TO FIND MY FRIENDS.
JUST POINT ME IN THE RIGHT DIRECTION.
AH! AH!
THANKS.

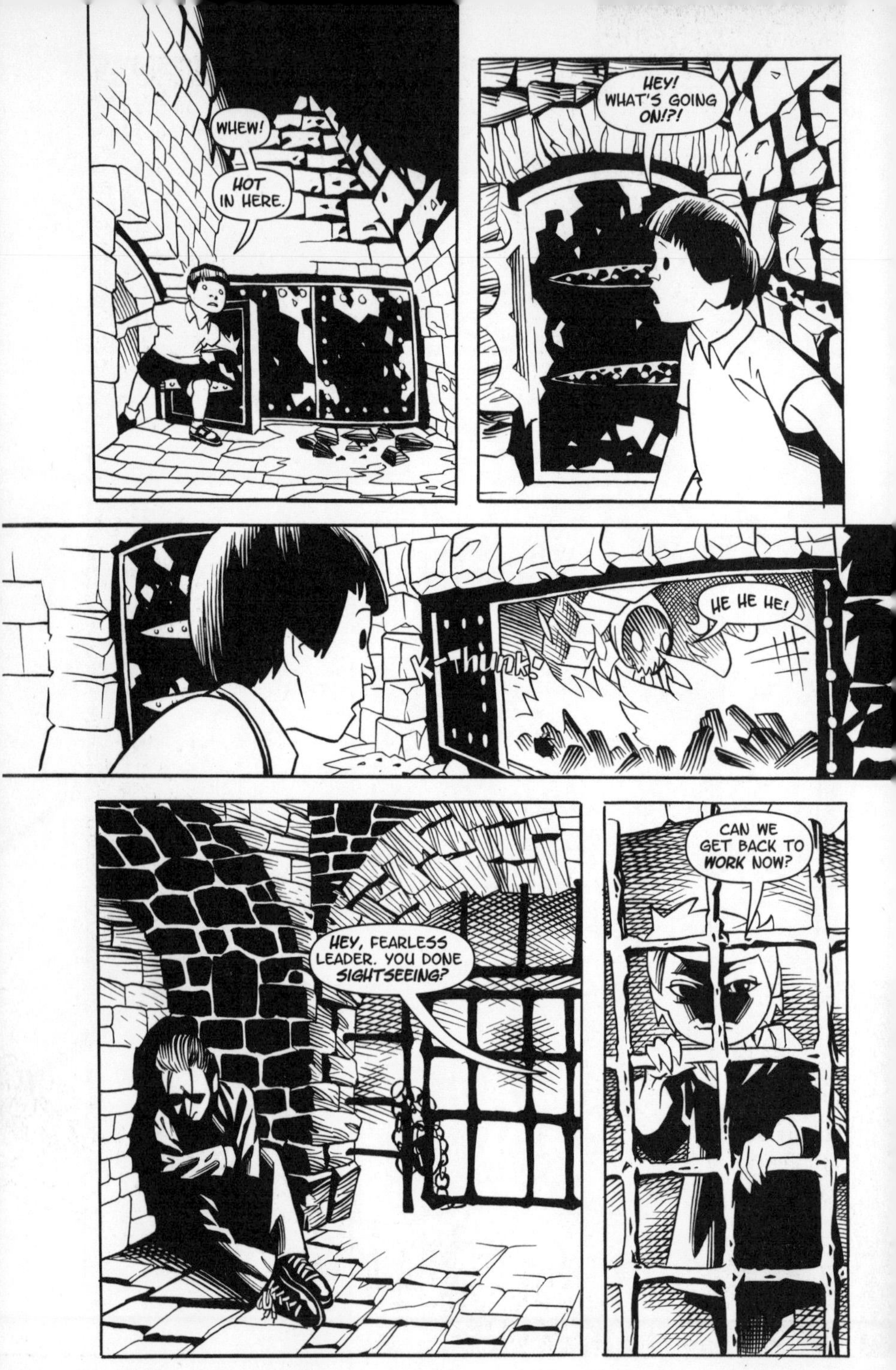
WHEW!
HOT IN HERE.
HEY! WHAT'S GOING ON!?!
K-Thunk!
HE HE HE!
HEY, FEARLESS LEADER. YOU DONE SIGHTSEEING?
CAN WE GET BACK TO WORK NOW?

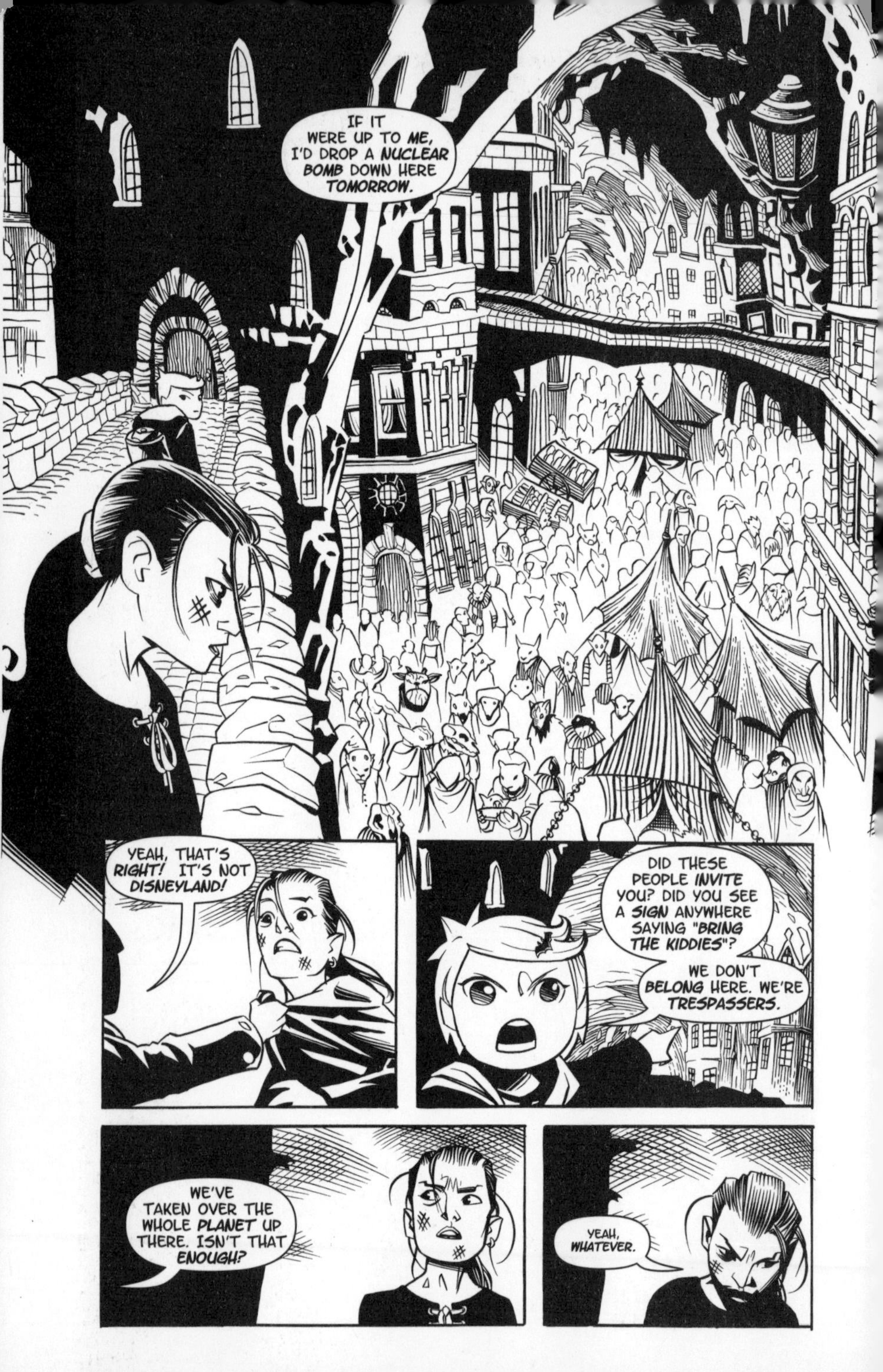
IF IT WERE UP TO ME, I'D DROP A NUCLEAR BOMB DOWN HERE TOMORROW.
YEAH, THAT'S RIGHT! IT'S NOT DISNEYLAND!
DID THESE PEOPLE INVITE YOU? DID YOU SEE A SIGN ANYWHERE SAYING "BRING THE KIDDIES"?
WE DON'T BELONG HERE. WE'RE TRESPASSERS.
WE'VE TAKEN OVER THE WHOLE PLANET UP THERE. ISN'T THAT ENOUGH?
YEAH, WHATEVER.

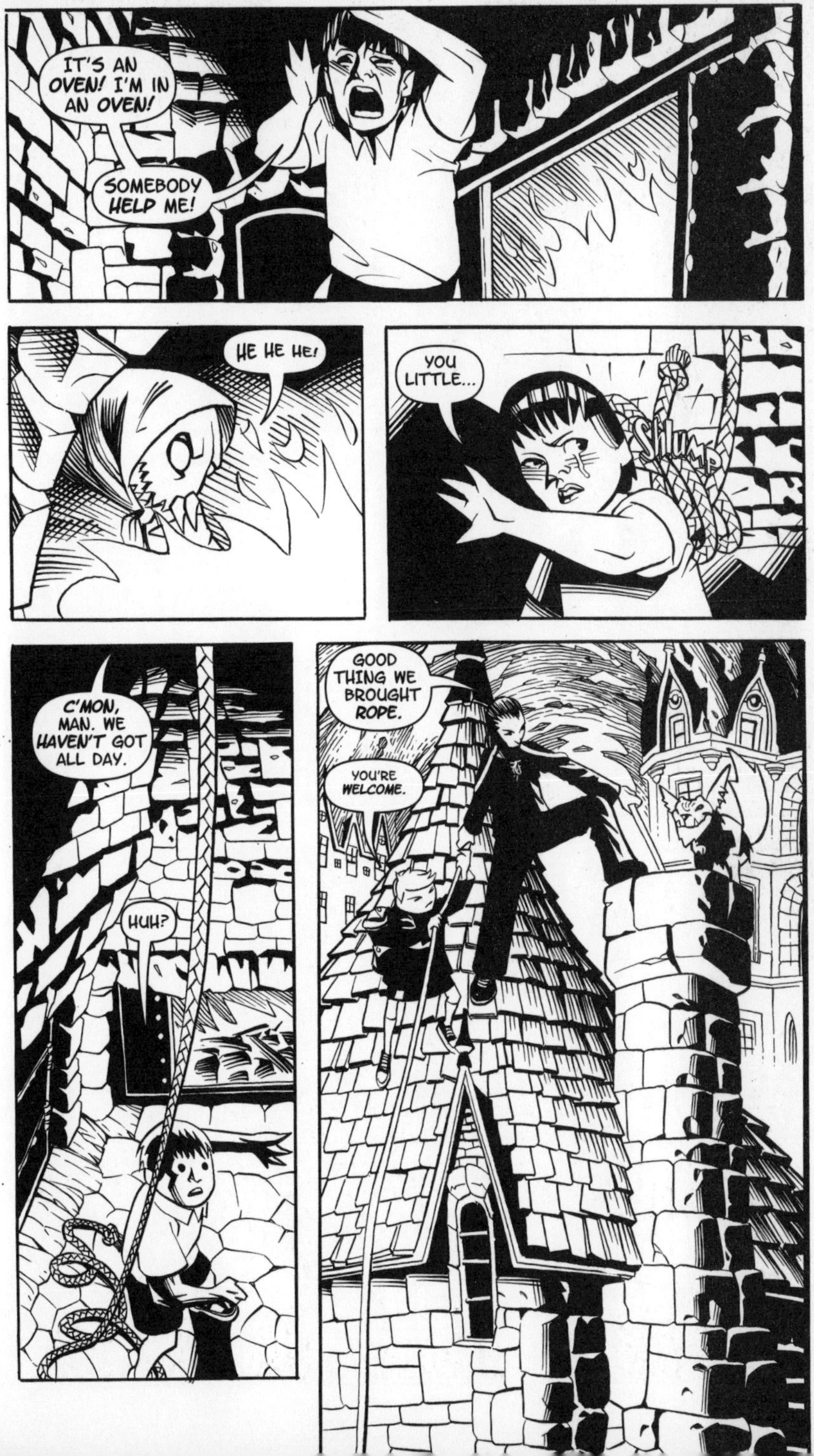
IT'S AN OVEN! I'M IN AN OVEN!
SOMEBODY HELP ME!
HE HE HE!
YOU LITTLE...
SHLUMP
C'MON, MAN. WE HAVEN'T GOT ALL DAY.
HUH?
GOOD THING WE BROUGHT ROPE.
YOU'RE WELCOME.

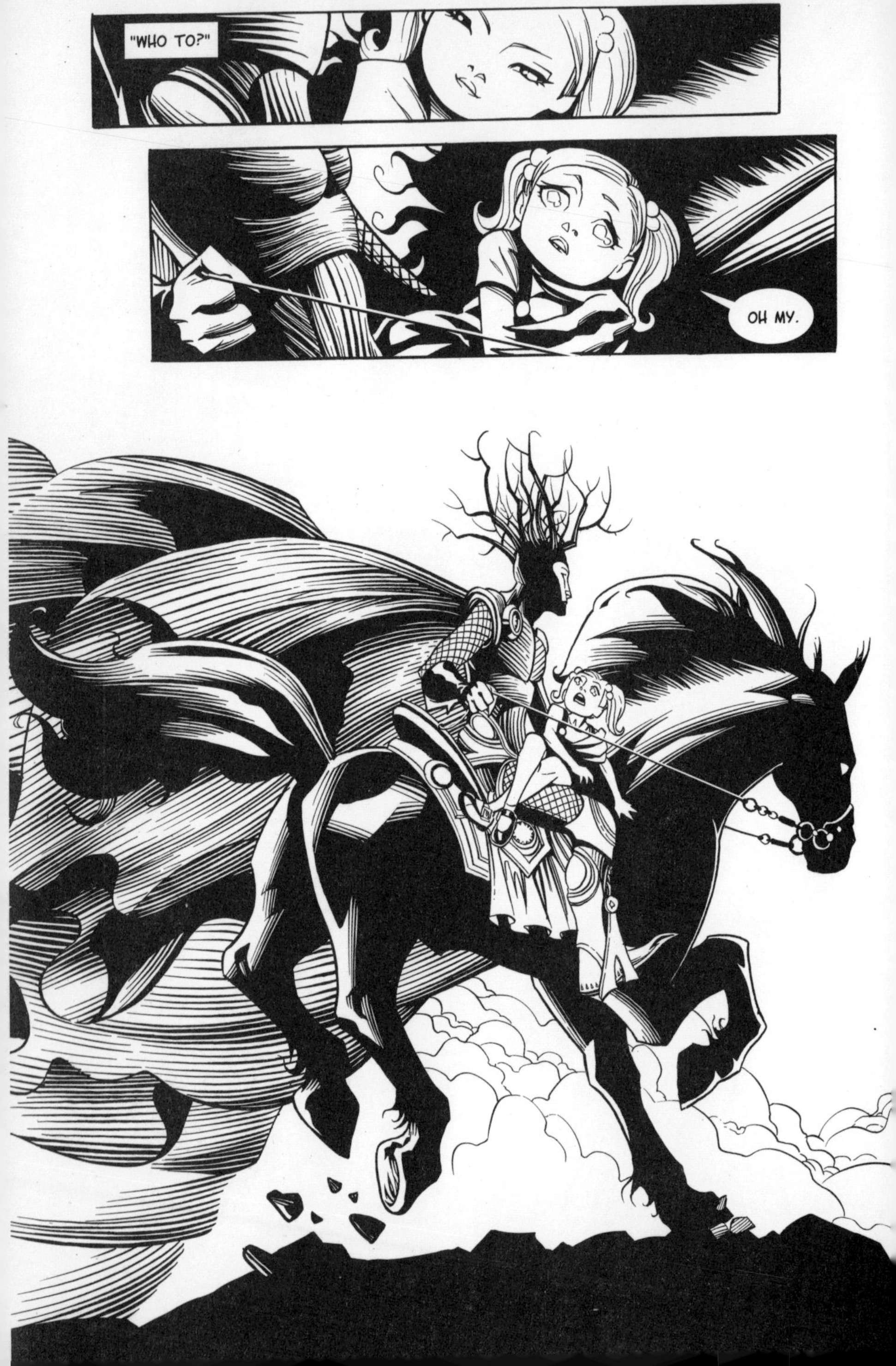
"WHO TO?"
OH MY.

CHAPTER FOUR

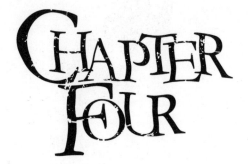

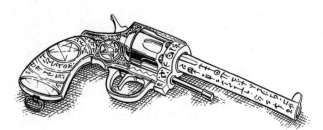

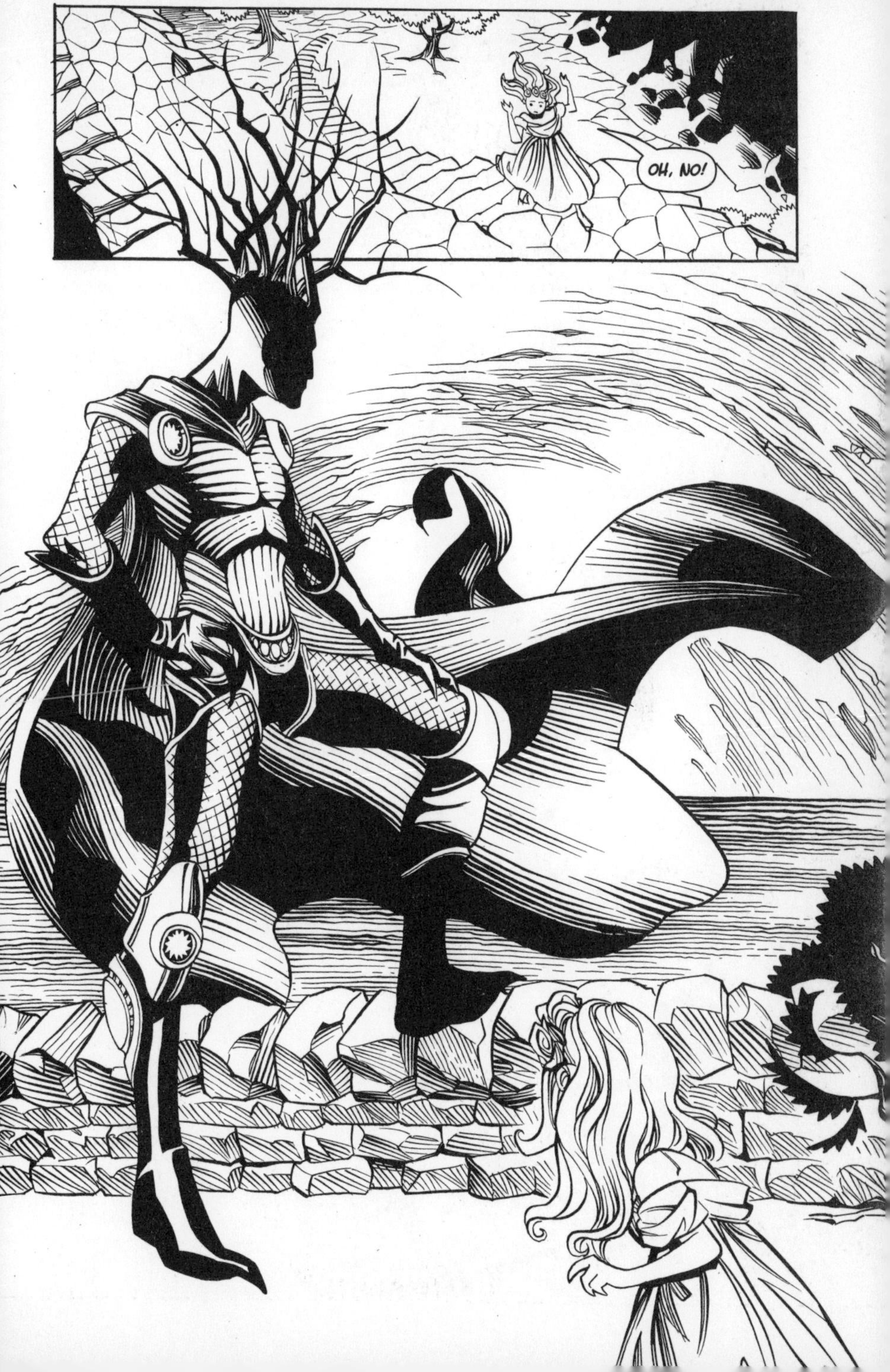
OH, NO!

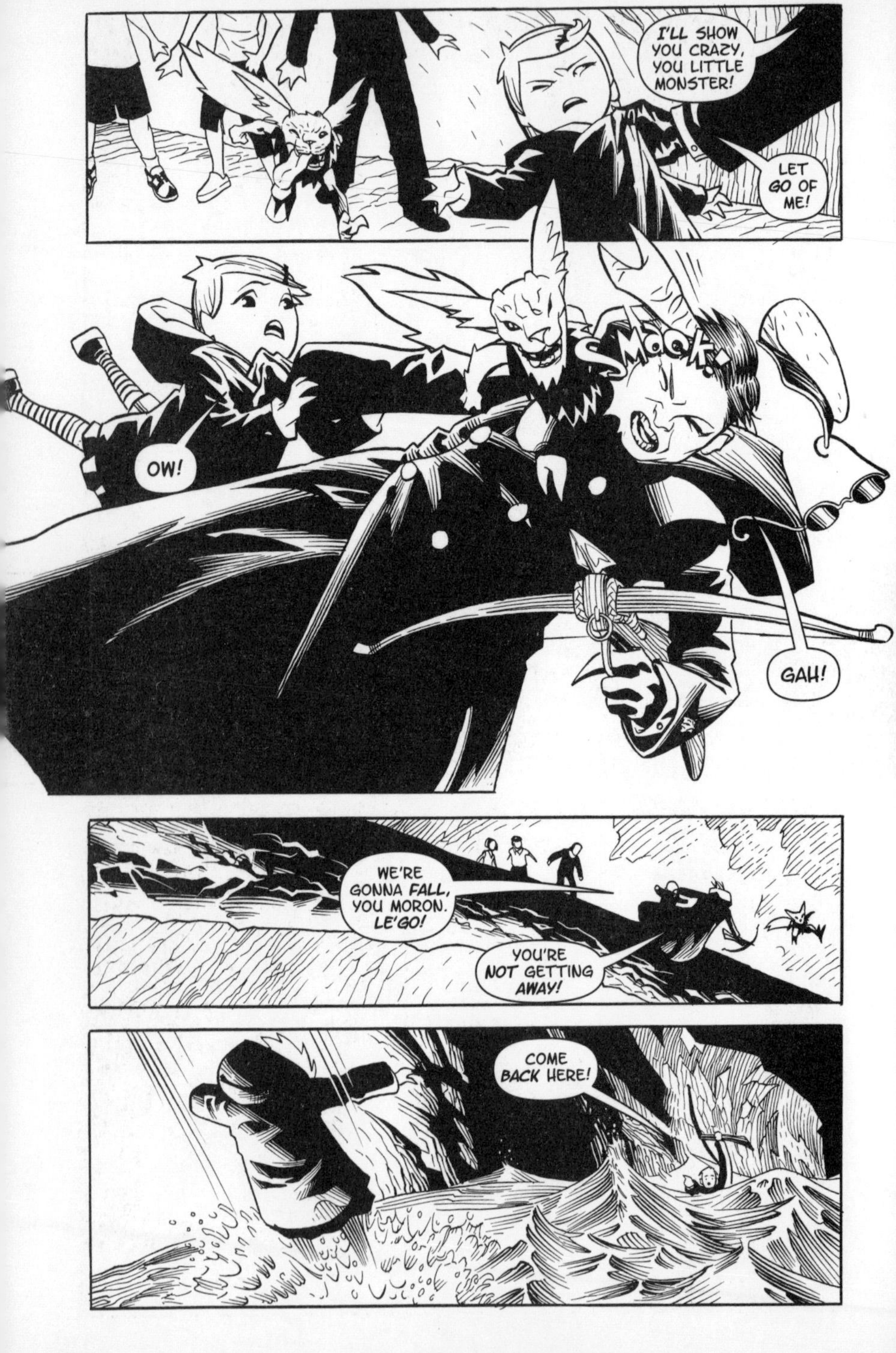
I'LL SHOW YOU CRAZY, YOU LITTLE MONSTER!
LET GO OF ME!
OW!
SMACK!
GAH!
WE'RE GONNA FALL, YOU MORON. LE'GO!
YOU'RE NOT GETTING AWAY!
COME BACK HERE!

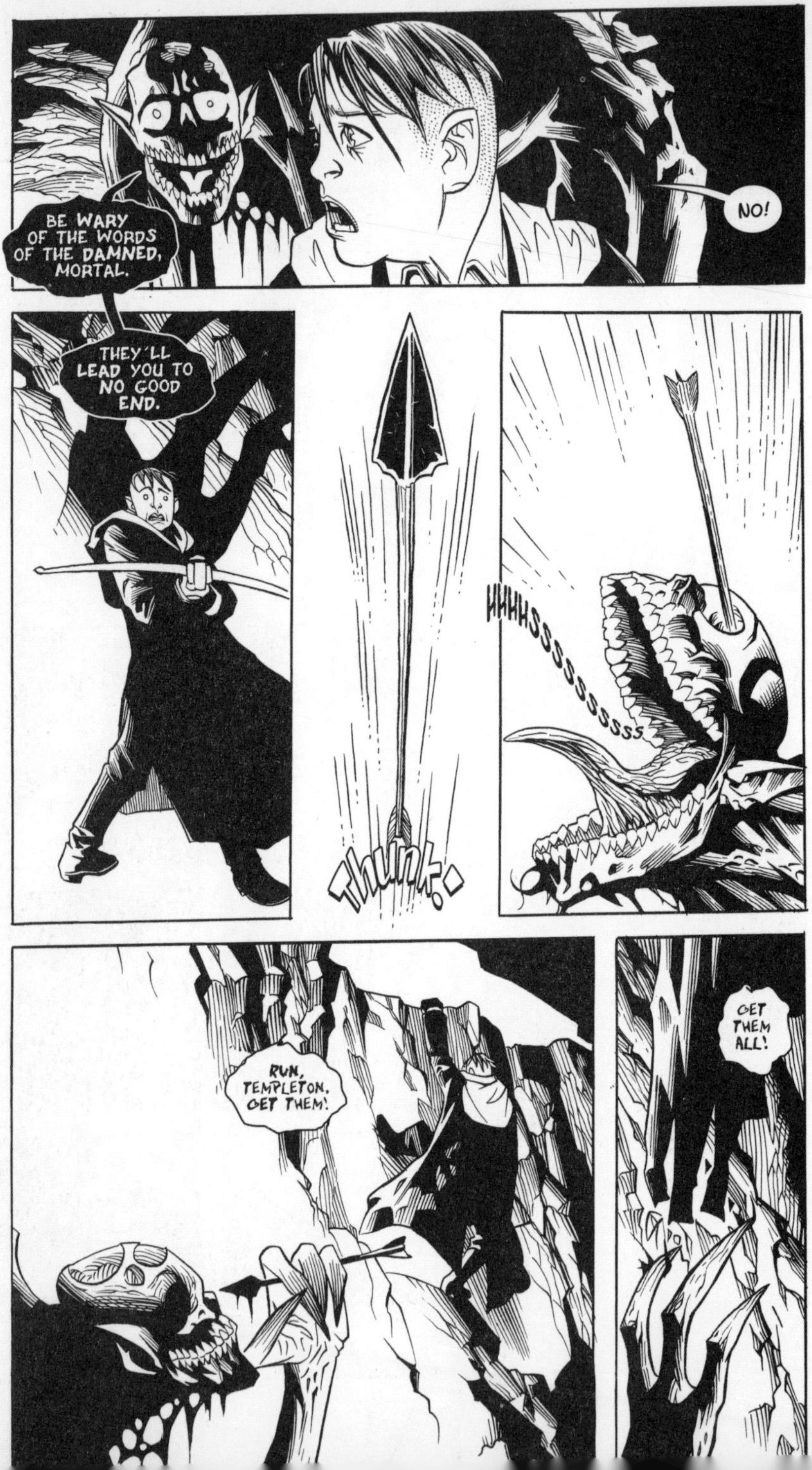
BE WARY OF THE WORDS OF THE DAMNED, MORTAL.
NO!
THEY'LL LEAD YOU TO NO GOOD END.
THUNK!
HHHHSSSSSSSSSSSS
RUN, TEMPLETON. GET THEM!
GET THEM ALL!

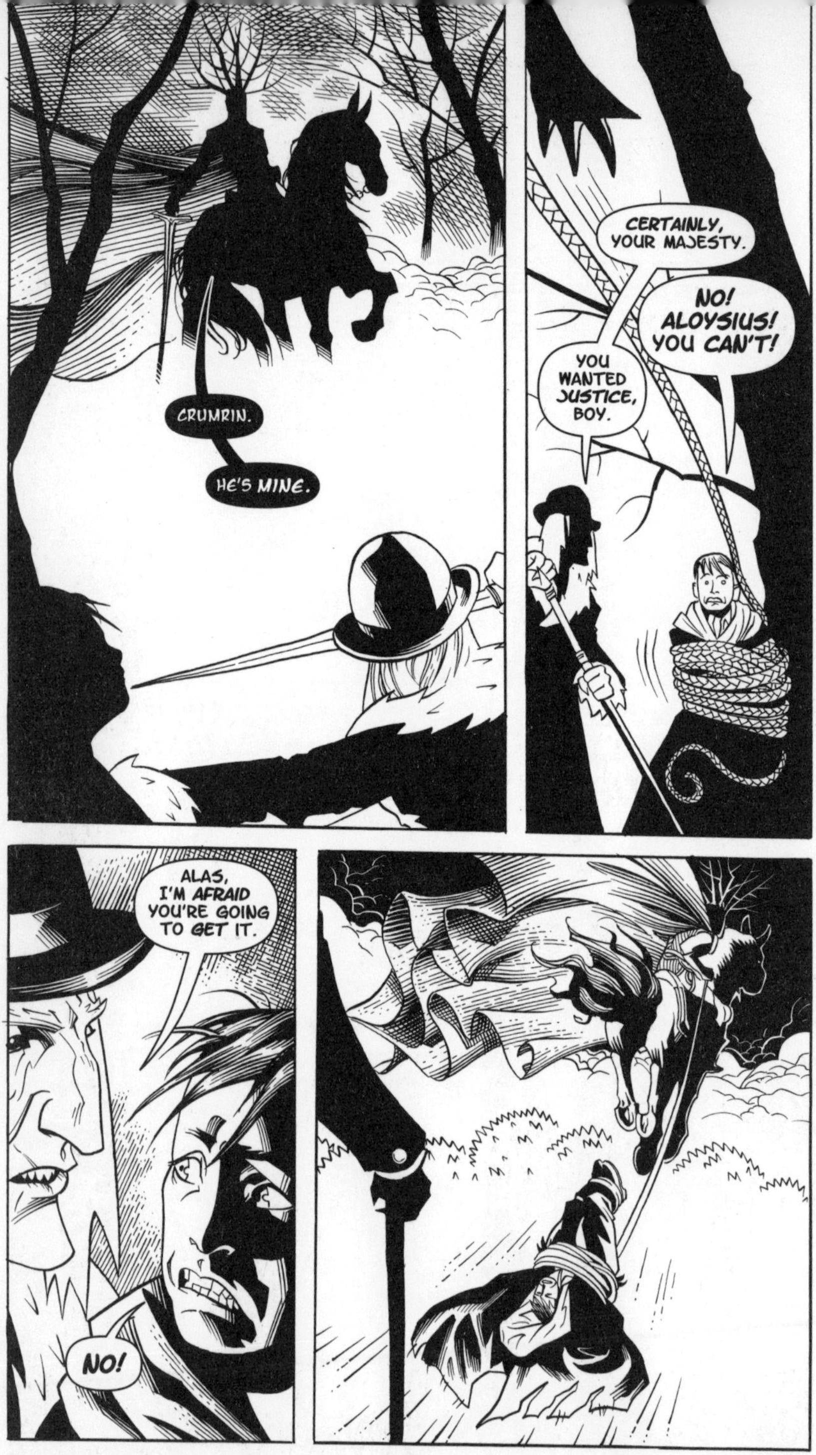
CRUMRIN.
HE'S MINE.
CERTAINLY, YOUR MAJESTY.
NO! ALOYSIUS! YOU CAN'T!
YOU WANTED JUSTICE, BOY.
ALAS, I'M AFRAID YOU'RE GOING TO GET IT.
NO!

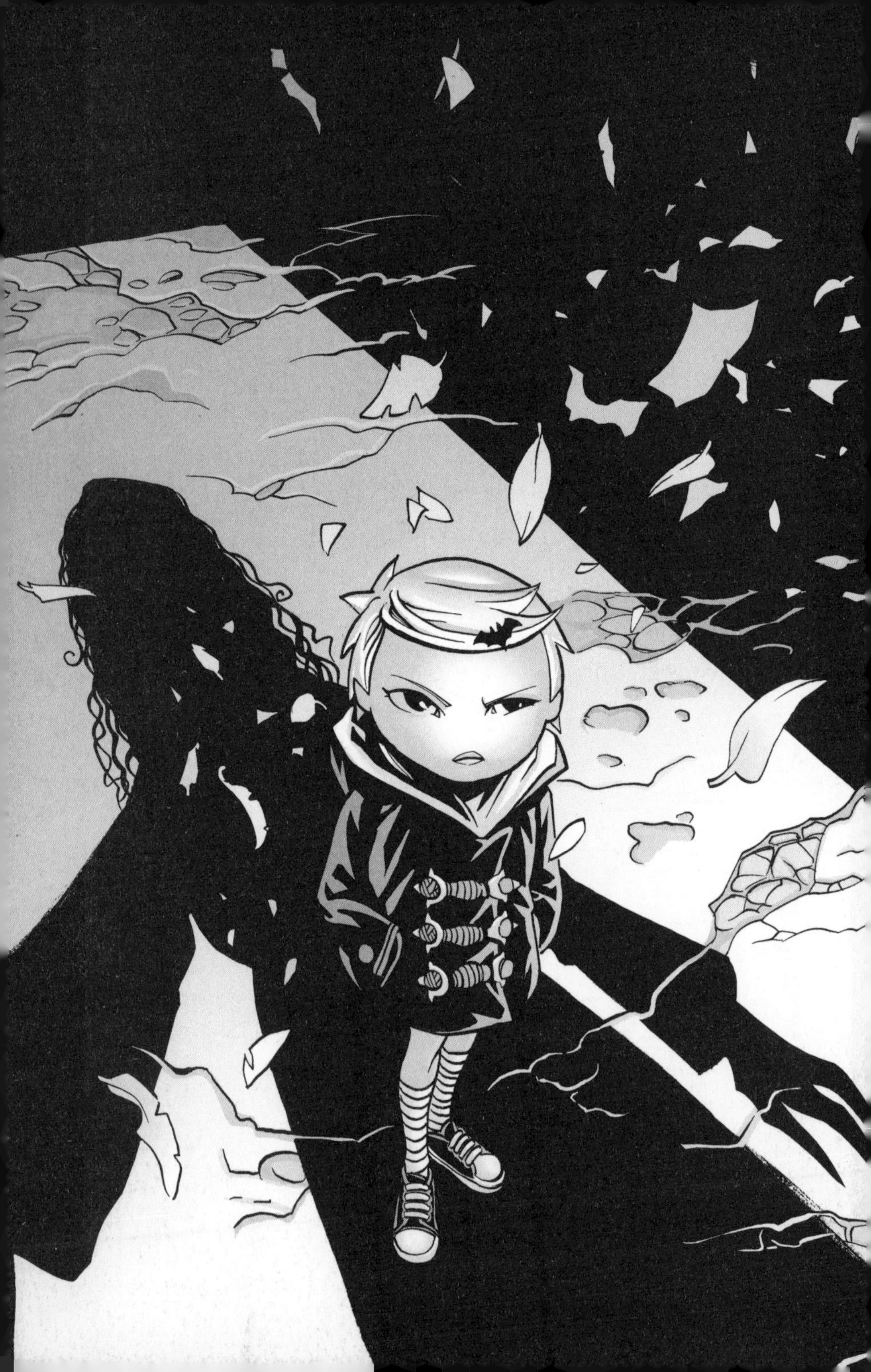

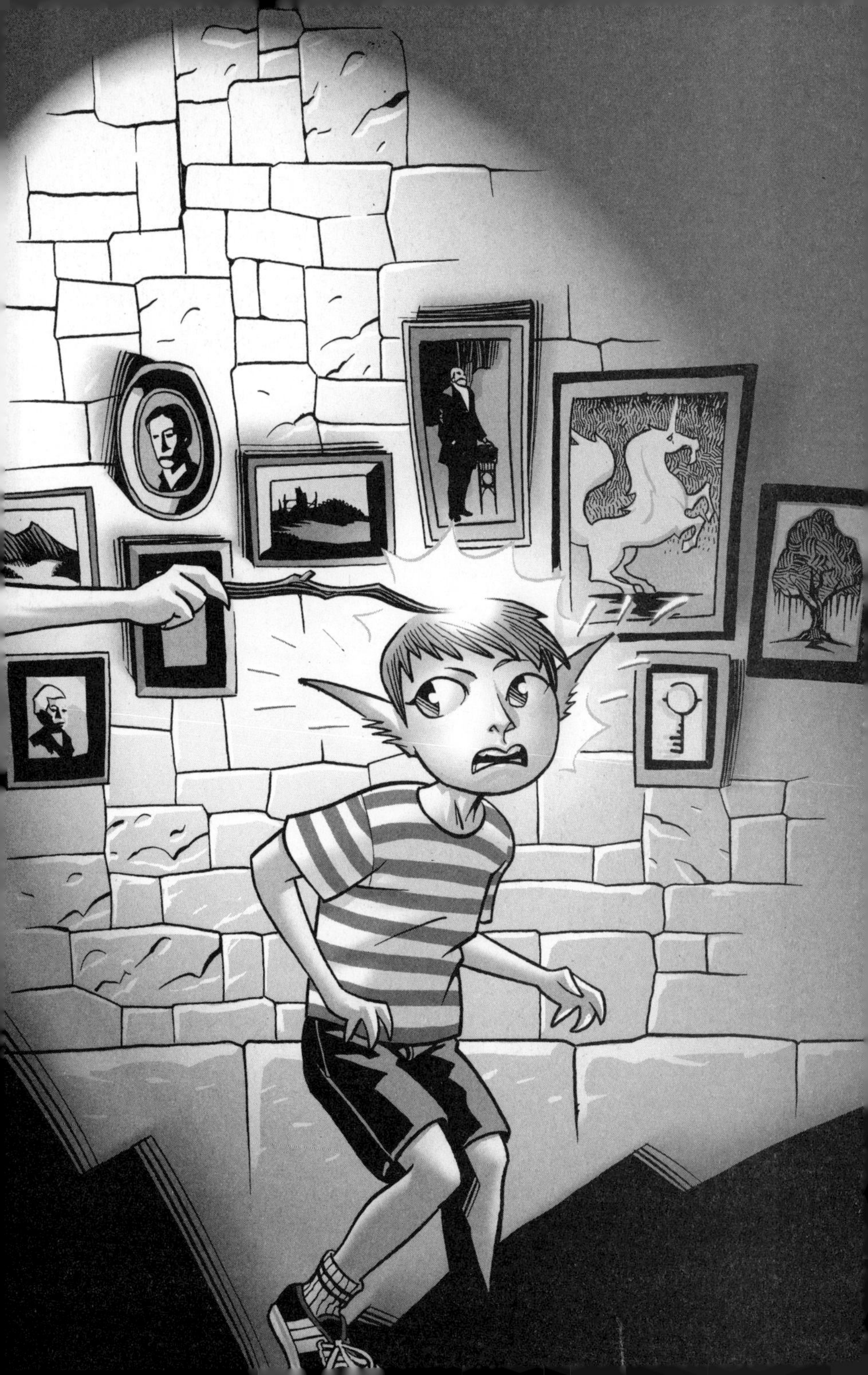

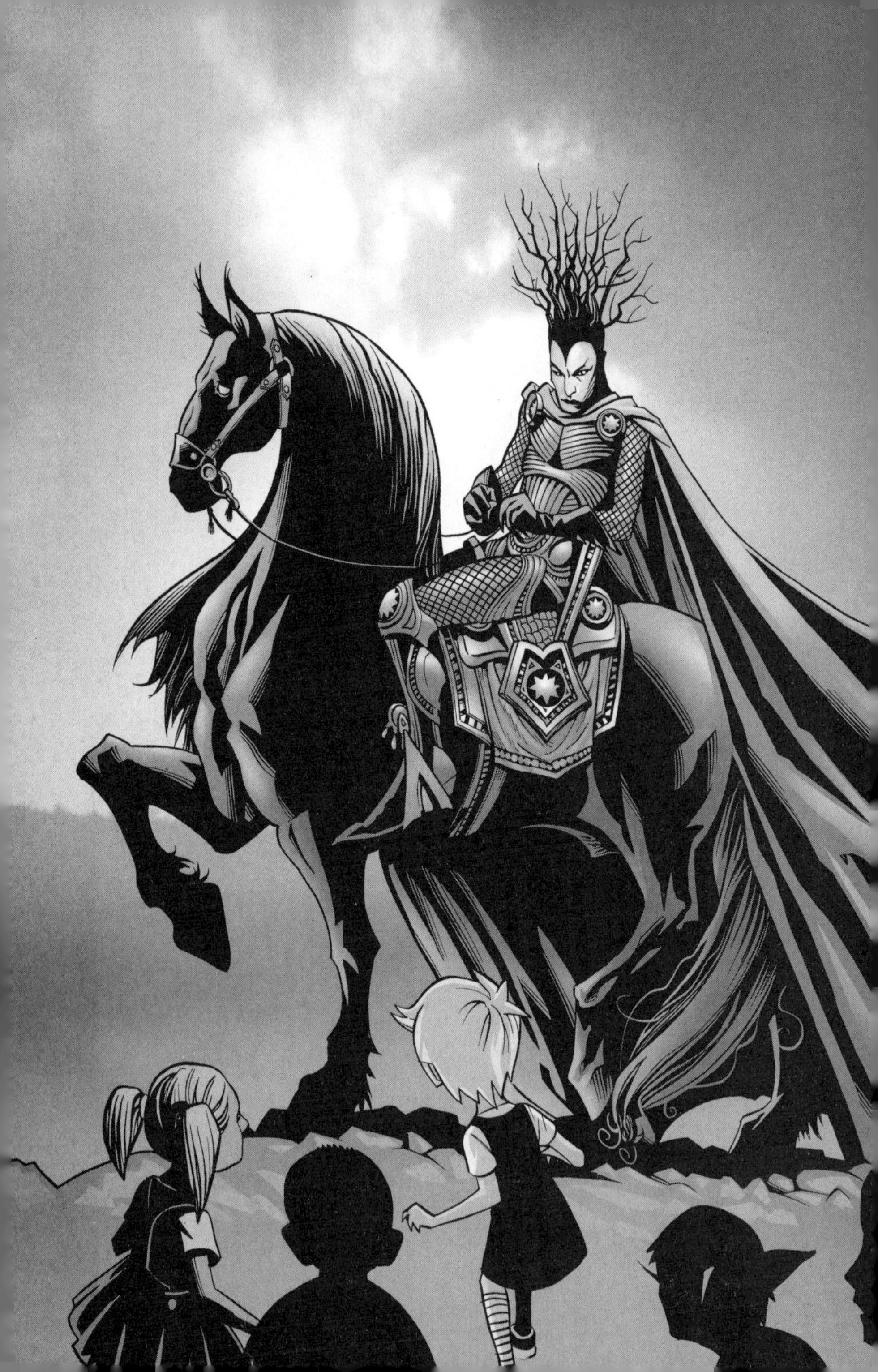

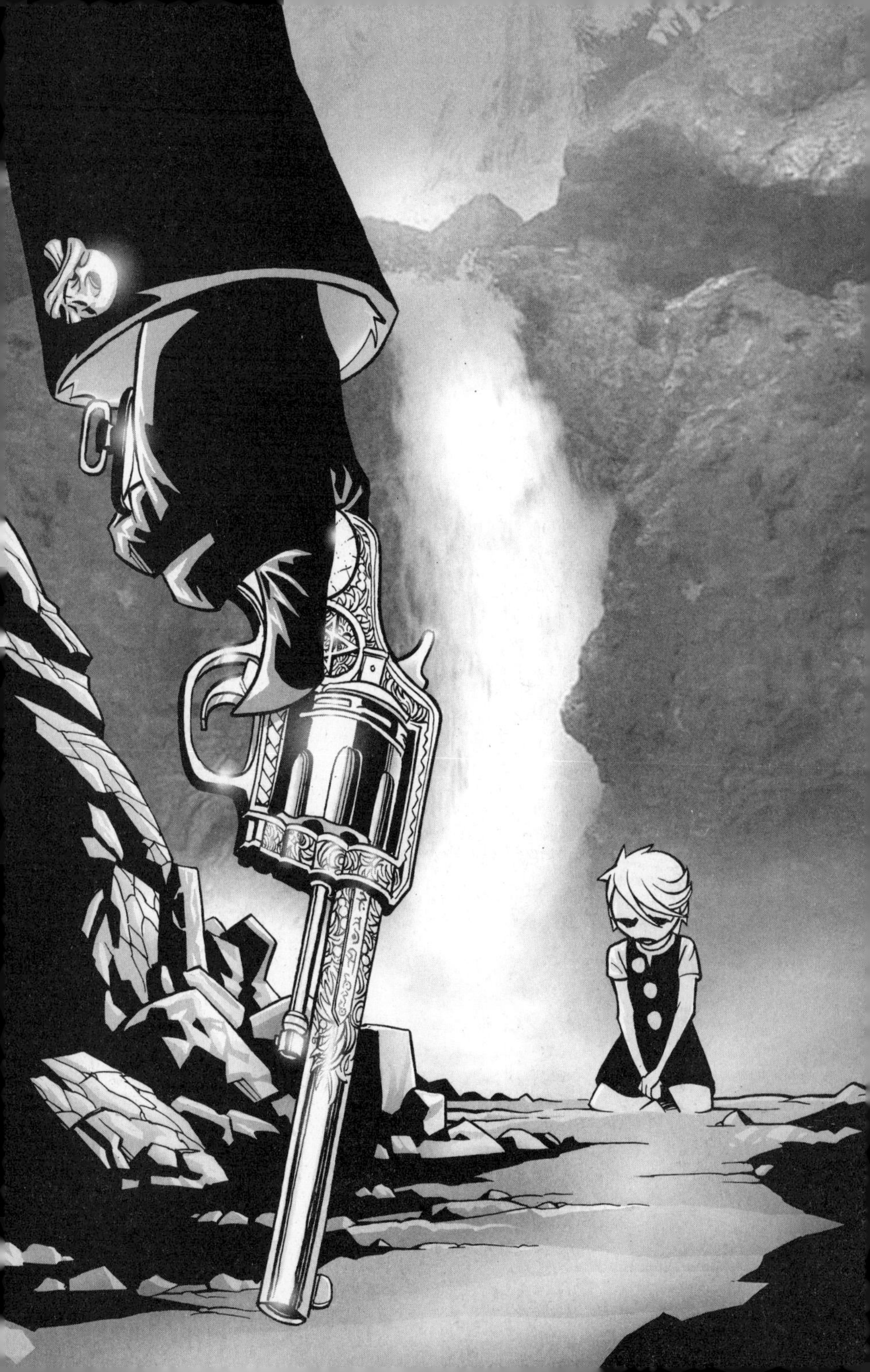

Among readers of the spookier sorts of comics, Ted Naifeh is a fan favorite. Since the early nineties, he's done illustration work for a wide variety of publishers, ranging from Marvel to Dark Horse to Wizards of the Coast. *Courtney Crumrin* represents his first published writing, and has been surprisingly well received. The original mini-series, *Courtney Crumrin and the Night Things*, was nominated for an Eisner award for best limited series in 2003.

Ted is also the co-creator of works such as the goth romance *GloomCookie* and the groundbreaking *How Loathsome*, now collected at NBM. He is currently starting work on his next project with Oni Press, the multi-volume fantasy epic *Glimmer*.

Ted resides in San Francisco because he loves fog.